Get Hired as Scrum Master

5th Edition

Dmitri Iarandine

Copyright © 2016-2020 Dmitri Iarandine

All rights reserved.

ISBN: 9781976768552

Contents – 1/2

1	Introduction	5
2	Agile Job Market Trends of 2020	9
3	Agile Delivery vs. Project Management	14
4	Job Transitioning Challenges	18
5	Understanding the Scrum Master Role	23
6	Scrum Master Role Hybrids	29
7	Obtaining Relevant Experience	39
8	Value of a Scrum Master Certification	46
9	Basics of Job Transitioning	50
10	Importance of a Great CV	65
11	Attributes of a Good SM CV	73
12	Scrum Master CV Template	84
13	Writing a Cover Letter	88
14	Cover Letter Template	93
15	Company Research	95

Contents – 2/2

16	Company Research	95
17	Preparing for the Interview	105
18	Collaboration Tools You Use	123
19	Conclusion	128
20	Other Books from JoinAgile	130
21	Feedback & Contact	134
22	About the Author	135
23	Copyright	136

Introduction

So you've decided to go ahead and change your professional title to a "Scrum Master", applying for one of those Agile job ads?

While the job market remains highly competitive in 2020 as I'm updating this book for the fourth time, I still believe that moving into the professional space of Agile Project Management and Digital Delivery is a great career development decision. This is due to the New Ways of Working movement remaining strong at least in Australia, and the Agile angle still being seen as the competitive edge over those professionals who are stuck in their solely traditional knowledge areas and methods of project delivery.

This of course comes from my slightly biased perspective of a person who started his career in Software Engineering, then transitioning into Agile Project Delivery space via a role of an Agile Business Analyst, and eventually getting to my goal of becoming a professional Scrum Master.

Currently I'm a Digital Transformation Lead, and an Agile Career Coach. I help large Australian organizations adopt the new ways of working, and work with the individual job seekers to increase their chances of being hired.

I'm not someone who entered the world of Agile from a classroom, but instead I've been fortunate enough to be given an opportunity to side-shift into an Agile role a lot time ago, learning "on the job", and pivoting my further career towards where I am now.

Formal education supporting most of professional job titles and roles these days remains important without a doubt, and as a person who obtained most of my early Agile experience "in the trenches" I had to loop back at some point, and fill my self-identified knowledge gaps with relevant training, certifications, and years of practice later.

Having said that, if I learned anything on my professional journey to becoming a Scrum Master and beyond, it is that practical experience doing the work of a Scrum Master, always outweighs any of the Agile certifications or academic qualifications you might have obtained earlier and decided to pin to your cubicle wall.

There are a lot of transitioning professionals and job seekers who are applying for that same Scrum Master job ad you are interested in, all with their own unique experiences, certifications, differently formatted Resumes, personal strengths and weaknesses.

This book is not a Scrum Guide, and its goal is far from teaching you Agile concepts and particulars of such things as Scrum Framework. There are plenty of freely available resources that you should have studied to this point that would do a better job explaining everything you need to know, saving me the time too.

Instead, the main goal of this book is to increase your chances of getting hired for a Scrum Master role if you applied externally, or what we call "from the street". Having no contacts or references within the company offering a job, you'll have to deal with all the usual hoops of the recruitment process.

This book was written to help you navigate that journey - starting from the latest insights into the Agile job market trends of 2019-2020, talking you through what you should expect as someone relatively new to our professional space, advising you on the basic format of your Resume, providing suggestions on how to handle most common Agile interview questions, and much more.

I'd also like to make it clear that this book is not about teaching you how to fake a facade of someone who looks like a Scrum Master, getting hired simply because they've fooled the recruitment process. I've met plenty of people performing certain jobs where I was wondering who hired them and how did they get there.

Let's not make you one of those!

What this book will help you with however is explaining the "rights" and "wrongs" of a good Scrum Master mindset that would lay the solid foundation for other improvements of your Persona as someone ready to go get that job.

The rest of helpful moves that will hopefully give you a winning edge over the other applicants will come as a secondary element of what I'll be trying to teach you in the following chapters.

As part of achieving this goal, there are a lot of things we'll need to cover, but fear not - we'll get through it all in the end.

It's worth pointing out that parts of this book will read like I'm giving you too much generic context, but this is my deliberate attempt to trigger the right mental state in yourself as a potential job candidate, transitioning into a very specific job market full of certain implicit rules and unsaid expectations.

You need to properly understand what those are.

Key Topics We'll Cover

The following chapters of the book will cover these key topics:

1. Understanding what a Scrum Master is really expected to do, versus the classic definition of the role in Scrum Guide;

2. What are the "Agile Hybrid Roles", and why should you be familiar with how to interpret their job description as you browse the job classifieds or recruitment websites;

3. Understanding the key challenges a Scrum Master job applicant is

going to face, when only just transitioning into the role. This will depend on your current or previous job title, and how well you've presented it in your Resume;

4. How to capitalize on your current skillset, choosing the best way forward when applying for one of those Agile roles, including Scrum Master;

5. What is considered to be the sufficient amount of experience that you need to have and demonstrate to the recruiters before you can hope that your Scrum Master job application will be successful;

6. How to best prepare your Cover Letter and Professional Resume, more commonly referred to as your "CV";

7. What to expect from a Scrum Master interview - this is where we'll look at questions that they'll likely ask you, and how to best respond to those.

I'm certain that you'll feel like a much better prepared Agile job candidate after reading this book and taking some of the tips on board.

Without any further ado, let's get started by quickly reviewing the latest Agile job market trends of 2020.

Agile job market trends of 2020

As I wrote and published this book in 2016, I felt the need to periodically revisit and update its content, keeping it relevant for the job seekers of the present day and age. Reflection of the latest job market trends is among some of the most helpful things I could share with you, as this information will help better navigate your job search and application efforts.

While a lot of facts this book tells you about the Agile job market in Australia remain the same in 2020, overall theme we've been witnessing over the past year or so was the increase in the number of people obtaining some sort of Agile certifications, and going straight ahead to apply for the most typically advertised Agile roles – your Scrum Masters, Iteration Managers and Agile Delivery Managers.

A couple of years ago we saw the job market dominance of what I labelled in this book as the "hybrid roles", as well as plenty of the entry level positions, such as the vague "Junior Scrum Master" or a little better defined "Agile Business Analyst".

I've even recommended that someone new to our industry and Agile Project Management space in general would try and seek those roles out as their initial career pivoting point – simply because securing those roles as a "foot in the door" used to be much easier than going straight up against the steep competition of higher qualified and skilled professionals who wanted the mantle of fully-fledged Scrum Masters and Agile Coaches.

In the late 2019 we saw fewer junior or "hybrid" roles advertised on the Australian job search websites, quite possibly due to the growing interest in all things Agile from many companies and job advertisers, with a lot of professionals transitioning into our space internally rather than via the open job market.

With a lot of large-scale Agile transformations under way across the Australian corporate landscape, the demand for junior or mid-level Agile roles grew exponentially, exposing the cheapest way for the companies to fill these roles by encouraging the expressions of interest from their existing employees, who in many cases got a "free pass" into the shoes of freshly baked Scrum Masters or even Agile Coaches.

I've personally witnessed such insane career leaps for many individuals who were severely unqualified to become actual Agile Coaches, but where the companies allowed those rather unsubstantiated and poorly supported internal promotions to happen. I'm not a fan of these trends as this effectively degrades the perception of Senior Scrum Master or Agile Coach title when broad ranges of people get exposed to the lacking contribution and skill levels that those unreasonably promoted people can demonstrate.

I'm a fan of progressive and deserved growth of any professional, that then gets appropriately reflected in their job title. This sentiment will remain a theme throughout this book, supporting my recommendations for you to seek step-by-step career progression, rather than hope to magically leap all the way to their desired position, while knowing all well themselves that they are not qualified to do the work yet.

Another related strong job market trend of 2019-2020 is the vastly increased demand for people capable of demonstrating and sharing their Lean-Agile knowledge as trainers and coaches.

While some larger corporations desperate for qualified resources might resort to the mindless internal promotion strategies I've just mentioned above, the shortage of more highly qualified Agile personnel remains noticeable on the market, as soon as you start talking directly to the recruitment professionals or hiring management.

What does it tell you?

Well, at the very least that investment into growing your professional knowledge of Lean-Agile methods — not just limited to Scrum Framework! — and seeking additional validation from professional certification bodies will help you differentiate yourself from the grey masses of look-alike job candidates with a basic Scrum Master certification.

Another trend worth considering and pointing out here is slow but steady re-labelling of what used to be known as Agile Transformations into Digital Business Transformations.

"Agile" as a term has burnt too many individuals and organizations out, due to excessive overuse and poor implementations that gave it a really bad name.

We've heard and cringed over the term *"FRAGILE"* in the past, but in 2019 this trend became almost a status quo, hitting senior champions of Agile – mainly Coaches and Trainers – pretty hard, asking for extra resilience and efforts to be put in defending our ways as those that still can work and deliver real value.

Digital and Business Transformation Coaching is now a more prominently emerging trend, just like Agile Coaching was a few years ago, meaning much broader influence as part of changing the culture, mindset and operational methods of the impacted organizations.

This field and self-labelling in professional sense means greater and broader responsibility and set of requirements that would be way beyond what I should realistically cover for you in this book.

But the knowledge of this general trend is undoubtedly going to be of some value to you as a career-pivoting professional who should at least remain familiar with the latest terms being thrown around on the job market.

Growing demand for Agile jobs from the interested applicants was easily predictable and visible even a few years ago, now resulting in generally worsened conditions for the people fresh to Agile job markets, and who didn't have any specific references or internal job transfers within their current companies.

Recruiters became even more overburdened with job applications and professional CVs from generally unqualified people, relying more on the growing range of automated pre-screening and professional competency testing systems – one of which was recently developed and released by our JoinAgile Initiative that you could learn more about in another chapter towards the end of this book.

So in essence, as with many other aspects of our modern lives – "the later you catch a train, the fewer seats will be left on it" – sentiment remains true, whether we like it or not. It's the same as with the investments in real estate, gold, Bitcoin, and stocks.

But once again I'll encourage you not to despair.

Yes, we all would have loved to be there in 2007 when Bitcoin cost under $1. But we were not – otherwise I wouldn't need to write this book, and you'd never become my reader!

Our professional response to this growing competition remains spread out between the following points:

1. **Remain competitive** and keep up the initiative – if you don't play, you'll never win;

2. **Develop yourself professionally** – information remains the power of our society, and reading this book is one of the points that differentiate you from those who don't;

3. **Learn how to grow your personal brand** in your professional space – as the world gets saturated with job applicants, the only naturally differentiating factor becomes YOU, rather than some certification that a million of other people possess;

4. Consider services of a Career Coach, especially if you don't have years of experience to put on your CV or convert into a more Agile-friendly language that would satisfy the hiring management. Our own JoinAgile Initiative offers such services should you be interested to visit our website and research if this is something that would help you further.

Agile Delivery vs. Project Management

Our professional space is most commonly known and referred to as "Agile Project Management". Individuals and hiring companies keep using this label as a universal wrapper around almost anything Agile-related, whether it's actually related to planning and delivering modern projects, or not.

Not trying to sound pedantic here, I thought clarification of the overarching term would be in order, as otherwise it's a bit misleading. I want to make sure we separate our domain sufficiently from the shadow of traditional Project Management.

I'll try and keep this around Scrum Framework and Scrum Master role to fit into the title of the book and not make this too broad, but in essence, **Scrum Masters are not Project Managers** and should not be covered by the same umbrella of terms.

Even the classic definition of Scrum Master role that comes to us from the Scrum Guide points out that the role is very different from a Project Manager; it has completely different professional agenda and methods of control in mind.

So I think paying attention to this difference and feeling like a Scrum Master rather than a re-labelled Project Manager when applying for one of those new roles would be the first step in the right direction as a successful job applicant for you.

I refer to our professional space as Agile Delivery, or *Digital Delivery*.

So what's Agile Delivery and its subset of job market really like these days?

It is really popular, competitive, and inflated by the job ads that get on average between 50 and 200 applications depending on the hiring company and the advertised pay grade.

This effect of the numerous job candidates swarming over those Agile job ads can be intimidating and rather depressing for most people who consider applying. Such demand creates a very forgiving ecosystem for poorly phrased or flat-out ridiculous job descriptions and requirements that the advertisers don't have to try and polish any longer, since the fruits of their poor labor are in high demand anyway.

I'd go as far as calling a lot of Scrum Master job ads sloppy - at least in the Australian market.

Among the other things that we'll start slowly unfolding and learning to handle better in the further chapters of this book, this effect of market unfriendliness for new job seekers is caused by these two major points:

1. The employers and recruiters who represent them vary greatly in their knowledge of Agile and understanding of what Scrum Masters are supposed to do.

While as the time passes there are naturally more and more of those who become better informed, adjusting their hiring expectations and how their job ads read, there is still a scarily high percentage of really badly defined jobs, polluted by mandatory lists of responsibilities a normal Scrum Master should never consider doing;

2. As already mentioned in the Introduction of this book, the job market is overflowing with applicants who see Agile Delivery and the whole Agile Project Management space as the new "place to be". Many also think that it's relatively easy for them to transition into these more popular roles by quickly backing themselves up with Scrum Master certifications and then starting to bombard the recruiters with their CVs.

Both of those factors lead to inflation of job requirements and the expectations of the hiring management. Looking at some of the job ads of late 2019 on LinkedIn or the local Australian job listing sites, I couldn't believe how openly obnoxious and ridiculously stretched the advertisers make those jobs sound.

And what makes things worse is the fact that they get rewarded by hundreds of people still applying for those ads, rather than ignoring them, and signaling back to the advertiser that what they ask for is beyond reasonable expectations.

I speak to a lot of recruitment professionals as part of the activities of JoinAgile Initiative and can assure you that they suffer from these effects too!

After all, let's not forget that the recruiter is often completely dependent on the demands and expectations of the company that pays them to find the people matching the job descriptions they've supplied.

While some companies are still open to the advice that some of the better recruiters try and provide as part of their services of a talent-seeking middle-man, a lot of advertisers just tell the recruiter a dream vision of who they'd like to find for their job, leaving them with an impossible mission to dig through the hundreds of applications to find someone close to the received description...

It's always been hard to find a dream job that you would love – even having some solid practical experience to support yourself with, but for the purposes of this book let's assume that you are new to Agile Delivery space, as a freshly certified Scrum Master, or perhaps someone who is only just considering to "jump ship", trying to size up what they are up against.

Before we begin talking more specifically about what those advertised Scrum Master roles practically expect from you, and what qualities we need to bring to the forefront in yourself as a potentially successful job applicant, let's take a quick high-level view at what exactly we are up against.

Job Transitioning Challenges

Any change is hard, at least for the vast majority of people.

What's even harder is to embrace a completely new mindset that the new role requires, figuring out how to change your self-presentation both on paper, when somebody looks through your CV, and in person, when you eventually get to talk to someone at a face-to-face interview.

We will be reviewing variety of those challenges throughout the book, rather than diving into deep analysis of those right now, simply because the latter won't be of any particular benefit to you. After all, you just need to know what are the main obstacles, and how to build yourself up to overcome those most efficiently, right?

Let's go through my list of the key job transitioning challenges that you need to be aware of and prepared to deal with.

The "Wall" of recruiters

Recruiters are the people who work for the hiring organization, focusing their efforts on finding the right candidates for the advertised job. They can be internal or external to the employer's company, but in the context of this book we'll mostly talk about the external ones - not like it would change the process that much from your perspective as the job seeker.

The role of a recruiter was designed to be that helping hand to bring both willing parties together, simplifying your life as a candidate looking for a job, and helping their Client organization to find someone suitable.

With all the facts I told you about the Australian job market of the last year or so, you wouldn't be surprised to hear that this perfect image of a helpful recruiter became quite distorted, and not as pretty as we'd all like.

As I keep referring to the Australian job market, I'll allow myself one last disclaimer that due to my geographic location and business partnerships I'm mostly aware of the latest developments in the Australian Agile job market, not claiming to be an expert when it comes to international recruitment or job placements.

I'd be honestly surprised though if the main points that I'll present to you in this book would be not applicable to the job markets outside of Australia.

In the job market of 2020, the recruiters are still interested in finding you a job, because you are still the Product they are selling to their clients.

And it works as intended for the most part if you have a lot of relevant Agile experience, great references, and clear examples of how you've contributed in a similar role somewhere else.

But for an entry-level Scrum Master job seeker who doesn't have much experience taking care of Agile teams, with a rough looking CV, and maybe a single "common denominator" Scrum Master certification everyone simply takes for granted these days the same recruitment situation would likely appear a lot more difficult.

As mentioned several times above, the current job market and demand for Agile people has turned the recruiters and hiring managers behind them into choosers, while the job seekers start resembling beggars more and more.

The endless flow of job applicants who need to get screened and often sorted out into that entry level candidate category creates the sense of job search fatigue and desperation, when many of us don't even get a call back.

Recruitment agencies try to differentiate themselves from one another, just like you and I do as individual job seekers.

Some try and establish personal connections with the best candidates who they – or their colleagues – have successfully placed in the past. This saves them the headache and hassle of digging through the freshly received CVs and instead they just reach out to their established database for someone who might just be tempted by the new job offer, with higher chances of success thanks to their track record.

These people promise their clients that the applicants they put forward are "the people they know", which has proven to be a successful candidate placement strategy in many cases.

Other recruitment companies remain "body-shops" that don't seek the roles they've been exclusively given by their clients, but instead work by volume – picking up the jobs advertised by their clients in a non-exclusive manner, among other competing recruitment companies, and seeking to generate a flood of applicants where the number rules will win. That is, based on the assumption that among a 100 of applicants at least one might be a star their client wants to employ.

As you hopefully start seeing by now, it is a competitive market all around – for the recruiters applying different talent-sourcing strategies, and for the growing pool of job seekers, who try and stand out from the crowd, but often running out of gas – motivation, persistence in their efforts, ideas on how to be different from 10 others who just have applied for the same job.

Having the right experience

Companies offering a Scrum Master role to the best candidate expect you to help them achieve their goals, first and foremost. Any other philanthropic agenda that they might have on their corporate Vision statement comes second, or third.

So without a shadow of a doubt you do need to possess and demonstrate the right experience and the knowledge of the applicable industry when applying for a particular job. Knowing the Scrum Framework and Agile Manifesto back to front should come without saying, as those are non-negotiable and foundational education blocks freely available to you on the Internet, without which you should never dare calling yourself a Scrum Master.

Company and industry research should not be overlooked either, and we'll talk about the right way of doing your research as well as preparing your CV and Cover Letter in the further chapters of this book.

We will also talk about recognizing your prior experience or skills that have some "conversion value" when presented as part of your aspiring Scrum Master profile. Because the bottom line here is that not many companies would ever hire a Scrum Master with only classroom training or the knowledge of theory behind them, and literally zero practical teamwork experience shown in their CV.

You'll need to find a way to highlight those elements to the recruiter or the hiring manager reading your Cover Letter and CV before you can realistically expect to get invited for an interview.

Interview process

The chance of meeting your potential employer face-to-face doesn't come every day, as there are plenty of obstacles to overcome before you get to that point, so you'd better be ready and not waste it.

While writing a book like this one is not the same as coaching someone face-to-face, taking into account their personal circumstances, strengths, weaknesses, prior experience and skills they could try and put to the forefront, I'll take you through what I'd generally suggest you to prepare yourself for.

As I sit on interview panels and speak with job applicants regularly for both coaching and hiring purposes, I'll be able to summarize a few points that in my opinion apply for the vast majority of hiring managers and interviewers, across the board.

This should serve as a solid starting point for you to start preparing for an interview in the Australian job market, even without someone making more specific and personally tailored suggestions as your career coach would.

Understanding the Scrum Master Role

When someone considers applying for a Scrum Master role this suggests that they have certain personal motivation to succeed in this process, which would undoubtedly start with you reading through the Agile Manifesto, and then reading the classic Scrum Guide through and through, several times.

As already mentioned, both the Manifesto and the Guide are seen as the non-negotiable cornerstones of any career development towards Agile roles, whether you'd like to become a Scrum Master, Product Owner, or play any other professional part of a Digital Delivery process utilizing Agile methods.

Let's briefly go through the key points from the Scrum Guide using it as a reality check:

If these don't sound familiar to you at all, put down this book, go and download the Scrum Guide and study it thoroughly before continuing to read the further chapters and expecting those to turn you into an appealing Scrum Master job applicant.

1. Scrum Master is a not a Team Manager, but a "Servant-Leader", who helps the team learn about Scrum as a framework, and start embracing the supporting principles and behaviors of agility.

Scrum Masters keep the team members within boundaries clearly outlined by the framework, until they start embracing the Agile culture and the mindset, understanding why certain things are asked of them and why the established Scrum process is working this way;

2. Scrum Master acts as a "Lite version" of an Agile Coach, finding opportunities to help the various stakeholders outside the Scrum Team better understand Agile principles of transparency and collaboration, explaining what interactions with the Team would help the most, without detracting from the Scrum-based delivery process.

3. Scrum Master works with the Product Owner to help change patterns of interaction with the Team, to reduce distraction and maximize the value in the form of delivered Product Increments;

4. Scrum Master helps the Product Owner refine the Product Backlog, ensuring that all the Backlog Items are formatted clearly, and are easy to understand by the Team;

5. Scrum Master facilitates any ceremonies where required, demonstrating to the development team members how things should work, and encouraging them to take ownership of the Scrum processes wherever possible.

6. Wherever possible, the Scrum Master would spend time with the supporting management representatives to ensure that their Scrum team is set up for success and any impediments that are outside of the team's direct control could be removed by the people in control of the environment surrounding their individual team;

7. Scrum Master helps a broad range of stakeholders within the organization to better understand Scrum, empirical product development, and seeing benefits of Agile Scrum adoption over time.

This could involve running educational sessions, or sharing helpful materials and links to the resources that the others could read through;

8. Finally, any Scrum Master is expected to be a team player who is not locked in their limited Scrum Team circle, but who is seeking to engage and work with their other agilists who might be present in their company – including fellow Scrum Masters or Agile Coaches setting the pace of the ongoing transformation towards the new ways of working.

But what does "Agile Coach Lite" mean?

I did use this rather non-standard way to describe some of Scrum Master's responsibilities above, and should explain further what did I mean by that.

Depending on the higher level transformation model applied to the department or the whole company that your Scrum Team falls into, there is usually separation in responsibilities of a Scrum Master and an Agile Coach that would be good for you to understand.

As I've published a separate book that dives into this topic more deeply and addresses the agilists who are trying to transition further – into the shoes of an Agile Coach – I'll try and keep it brief here and only tell you that an Agile Coach has broader responsibilities than a Scrum Master.

A typical and non-hybrid Scrum Master is a delivery role. It means that they take care of their Scrum Team and limit their teaching to what Agile Manifesto summarized and how Scrum Framework wants the team to work. The purpose of Scrum Master's existence is to ensure that their team works as smoothly as possible, delivering value at regular intervals while inspecting and improving themselves in the process.

A typical Business Transformation Agile Coach is a meta role that is responsible for establishment of the right practices at all layers of the affected organization, not just the team level. Agile Coach is less focused on the delivery aspect of individual teams, and is more concerned about introducing and observing the right behaviors that will lead to creation of the right culture across the whole organization.

Agile Coaches are usually well-versed in the Lean-Agile frameworks and methods other than Scrum. They can assess the nature of work that the team is dealing with, recommending alternatives to Scrum-based delivery. Something that would be well outside of the responsibilities of a Scrum Master.

So when I say "Agile Coach Lite" when referring to a Scrum Master, I'd like to be clear that a Scrum Master does some educational bits and pieces of work that an Agile Coach would do in their stead if they were exposed to the lifecycle of an individual Scrum Team.

If you'd like to learn more about the differences between a Scrum Master and Agile Coach, and how to change your mindset towards starting to coach people at a higher level, you might find my book *"Agile Coaching: Where to start?"* helpful.

Going back to the reality of the present day Agile job market, the picture-perfect definition of Scrum Master role has actually changed into something very different from what the baseline of the Scrum Guide offered us years ago.

The employers lacking their understanding of Agile methods and culture, who are also spoiled by the volume of job applicants throwing themselves mindlessly at their poorly written "Scrum Master" job ads, start expecting their eventually hired Scrum Master to do lots of things that either contradict the whole definition of a Scrum Master role, or simply expand it unreasonably.

This is where the "hybrid roles" that I've mentioned above get born.

For better or worse, in the present day and age a Scrum Master needs to be accepting of those custom angles and hybrid responsibilities, if they want to get hired for most advertised jobs.

Having said this however, I'll say again that in my opinion any good *agilist* and Scrum Masters specifically should recognize when the employer's expectations start clashing with what we stand for, saying no to the attitudes and responsibilities that contradict the Agile principles at their core.

We will discuss some specific examples of those red flags that you'd need to look out for in the next chapter, but here I'll only encourage you to try and be on the same page with your recruiter or the hiring manager about the role expectations and reporting lines.

Scrum Master job descriptions vary greatly from company to company.

Not paying attention to the job description, only reading the advertised job title and hitting that "Apply" button could mean more trouble or embarrassment for you in the long run.

For example, not long ago I've seen an ad where among the mandatory requirements for a Scrum Master role the hiring company listed the *"Ability to dissect work into manageable chunks for the Team to work on - creating Product Backlog"*.

Requirements like the one above should make the eyes of any applying Scrum Master roll in disbelief, as those people clearly wanted to get a Product Owner or an Agile Business Analyst and the Scrum Master as part of the same package!

I will deliberately leave this topic for discussion in the next chapter, where we will talk about so called "Agile Hybrid Roles", that specifically ask for you to sit on multiple chairs as a "Scrum Master".

And in many cases being a hybrid is acceptable as a lesser evil, however being in control of this situation and understanding exactly what you are buying into as the job applicant should in my opinion be more important than getting hired for that job in the first place.

Doing your homework and researching more about the environment you are potentially looking to join as a new Scrum Master should be among the very first things to do, rather than jumping into the muddy waters headfirst. You will thank me later!

Misunderstood or otherwise unsupported role of a Scrum Master often turns into a nightmare either for yourself, or for the team, or for your employer.

Being able to spot the warning signs of trouble you might be walking into as a successful Scrum Master job applicant is one of the things I hope to teach you as part of this book, in the further chapters.

Deciding to **not apply** for a particular dodgy-looking Scrum Master job will be immediately more beneficial for you in some of those troublesome cases, compared to wasting your time, going through all the hoops of the recruitment process, just to eventually understand that you were never set up for success at all.

Scrum Master Role Hybrids

In all honesty, I probably should have kept the title of this chapter as *"Agile Hybrid Roles"*, but then I suppose staying focused on Scrum Masters will allow us to stay on topic and not go off too far into talking about broader "Agile Roles".

As I mentioned in the previous chapter, classic understanding of what a Scrum Master is hired to do could be very different if you simply ask hiring managers and other decision-makers from different organizations.

Knowing what the recruiter wants to hear before passing you through the initial screening filter applied to all of the applicants is critical to proceeding to the next stage - provided that you'd want to proceed, after learning more!

To make things even more complex for you, not all the recruiters simply re-post the Job Description they've received from their Client company that wants to fill a vacant position.

Some of those middle-men add their own spin to the job description, rewriting it for the job ad, because any of the following could be true:

1. They think they know better what the employer needs, because they specialize in recruiting Agile professionals, and the company offering the job is not.

Even when that assumption is correct, and the recruiter actually knows more about the Agile role domain and the candidates in general, it still may result in an artificial overhead of requirements that they put in front of candidates, without those skills or qualifications actually being needed by the employer;

2. They are already overloaded by the good quality candidates and impressive CVs.

They might be bound by the formally required duration of a job advertisement – that often applies to the Australian government or not-for-profit jobs – and keep the door open for the new applications, but inflate the requirements either in writing or verbally, when briefly speaking with the applicants over the phone.

Seeing the job ads updated towards the end of the advertising period to inflate the requirements and attract higher quality applicants or filter out those who would feel like the company is asking for too much is rare, due to legal and administrative issues this could cause. But hearing the recruiter becoming more difficult or picky towards the end of the job advertising timeframe, where they almost sound reluctant to talk to you, or doubtful of your qualifications is happening rather frequently.

Before we go through the actual hybrid roles, red flags to look out for and such, I'll make here a generic suggestion that it often pays to be among the first 10-15 job applicants before you start falling off the first page of the recruiter's application processing system.

While it wouldn't guarantee that you'll be reviewed or taken more seriously than the other applicants, I've personally dealt with a few cases where it was evident that the first 20 were given a lot more attention than the barrage of those who were late to the party.

It's a simple case of the recruiter or hiring manager filling their quota of those who fit the job description – which, let's be honest here, is not the hardest shopping list when it comes to hiring a Scrum Master – and not needing to keep reviewing the new applicants dropping into their inbox.

Be among the first, take any chance to increase your chances of being reviewed and hired!

Now, let's finally review the specific hybrid role titles that you could expect a Scrum Master job to mutate into in the present day and age. As mentioned above, some of these are acceptable mixes of responsibilities in my personal opinion, while others should be a clear sign of trouble for you.

Iteration Manager / Scrum Master

Iteration Manager (IM) is a broader and more loosely defined role title, which is actually quite popular in the Australian Agile job market.

While often an Iteration Manager would be seen as a Scrum Master, with no evident differences in their expected responsibilities, I suggest to see the role of an IM as a superset of a typical Scrum Master.

As the title of an "Iteration Manager" doesn't point directly at Scrum framework, it's open to a much wider interpretation by the employers, and is very often seen as a "Delivery Lead" or someone who is looking after more than one Agile team.

Those teams are commonly expected to work loosely following the Agile principles and practices, where the guiding rails are typically taken from Scrum, but in my experience these environments are often aware of their hybrid approach, rather than a properly established and formal Scrum practice.

In these work environments the Agile teams are expected to deliver value over the increments of time (Sprints), basically following a pattern of iterations, hence the role title. Management's awareness of their poor team composition, funding models, interference of Business-as-Usual activities (BAU), lack of Business buy-in or participation in Sprint Reviews and other activities however could all contribute to their desire to use a looser role title of an IM.

Knowing of these particulars and typical role naming patterns should give you some information that would allow educated guessing of what it would be like to work in a place like that, should you get hired for an IM/SM role.

To make sure you don't bite off more than you can chew when applying for an IM/SM role, it would be a good idea for you to try and confirm with the recruiter:

1. If this hybrid role title is referring to Iteration Management of the multiple Scrum Teams, as opposed to be focused on optimizing Scrum process for a single team;

2. Iterative Product delivery of the company you want to join might be actually not done the proper Scrum way, most likely representing some sort of Scrum derivative, perhaps adopting elements of Scrum, and otherwise running what's often negatively referred to as "Fragile";

3. Regardless of the delivery method adopted by the company, the Iteration Manager is often expected to perform some form of Project Management duties, such as attending steering committee meetings and providing project delivery updates in the format that is expected by the traditional layers of the organization.

If this in fact is the expectation of the employer, you need to be clear and content with performing such duties while trying to grow as a fresh agilist. There will be a guaranteed trade-off of getting hired for a job versus landing in an environment that's actually about Scrum and agility, and the new ways of working.

As always, it'll be down to your choice of how far off the beaten Agile track you'd like to take your career.

Scrum Master / Project Manager

Scrum Master / Project Manager (sometimes seen advertised as "IM/PM" too) hybrid roles are without a shadow of a doubt your worst nightmare, that might be hard to spot initially if you are getting desperate to get hired for your first "Agile job".

Let me try and explain why you'd want to steer clear from those.

Going back to how advertised jobs appear on the market, employers are usually providing recruiters with a Job Description (JD), specifying what is it exactly they want their new staff member to do.

Combining responsibilities of a SM (or IM) with those of a Project Manager demonstrates fundamental misunderstanding of what a Scrum Master is there to do, and how Scrum works, based on empiricism and relinquishing of direct control over how the work gets done and how delivery commitments are made. This inevitably translates into trouble for a successful job applicant, especially the one true to the concepts of Scrum and Agile in general.

A good Scrum Master is about "power to the people", coaching them about collaboration and transparency, iterative delivery of value, evaluation of progress made and feedback received, followed by necessary adjustments to maximize value of the Product during future Sprints.

Project Managers at a very high level are about attempting to establish and maintain control of every aspect of the Project that was sized, approved, funded and signed off for on the dotted line of precisely committed scope.

Project Managers try and create absolutely predictable result, maintain solid timeframes, report on exact budgets, and the other usually immovable constraints applied by the traditionally managed Program of work.

Project Managers have different toolsets, reporting expectations, metrics, and I'm yet to see a large enough number of a pseudo-Agile DSDM framework practitioners on the market to be convinced that a traditionally trained Project Manager can embrace Agile delivery without having to change their outlook on things.

It is certainly possible for a Project Manager to embrace the new ways of working through retraining themselves and being exposed to Agile Project Management and delivery methods for a while, but asking someone to be a PM and a SM (or IM) at the same time is utter nonsense, in my opinion.

As a result of accepting such role, you are likely to not succeed in either half of that hybrid, being torn between multiple fires, priorities and conflicting responsibilities, hardly learning anything and not establishing a good name for yourself in this new professional area.

Business Analyst / Scrum Master

Business Analyst (BA) / Scrum Master hybrid roles are very common on the market right now, because of largely interlinked and overlapping responsibilities, in small to medium-sized professional environments.

Large corporations and Scaled Agile Release Trains usually have the headcount and budgets to afford dedicated roles, where they don't need to combine responsibilities that a certain person plays purely from a budgeting perspective.

BA being a role not formally recognized by the Scrum Framework is very much alive as part of Agile Delivery within most of Australian companies that I had the pleasure of working for.

BA is often required as that additional "wrapper" that a lot of companies put around their Development Teams that Scrum Master is looking after. Business Analyst also works with the Product Owner, helping them define the requirements, capture them in the form of User Stories, refining the Backlog as a continuous and never-ending exercise.

In the case of the employer extending BA responsibilities into the more specific role of a Scrum Master, you are facing expectations of also looking after the proper understanding of Scrum as a framework and essence of the adopted Digital Product Delivery process.

You will be likely expected to facilitate Scrum events, organize recurring meeting room bookings and invites, being there to resolve impediments, and coach the involved parties on the best practices of Scrum and Agile in general.

Added requirements don't seem to be too overwhelming, and natural overlap of responsibilities looking after the health of Team's Product Backlog and how the work flows through the timeline of a Sprint makes this hybrid role a lot more sensible than what we've reviewed above with Scrum Master / Project Manager …

This overlap of responsibilities and closer familiarity with the artifacts of Agile Scrum also makes potential transition from a full-time Business Analyst into an SM role the easiest exercise of all we'll be reviewing very shortly.

Scrum Master / Agile Coach

It is one of the core responsibilities of a Scrum Master to educate the team and the Business stakeholders on Scrum practices and carry the flag of Agile forward where the relevant educational opportunity presents itself. So as it was mentioned above, Scrum Master is already expected to play a role of "Agile Coach Lite", as one of their out-of-the-box duties.

Being a full-time Agile Coach as a superset of Scrum Master's knowledge and expertise is something else entirely.

Specific request of your potential employer to combine responsibilities of a Scrum Master with an explicit call-out to Agile Coaching duties could tell you a lot of things about the organization you might end up working for.

1. The hiring organization explicitly advertising for Agile Coach role even in a hybrid capacity of a Scrum Master, is likely to be more mature in their understanding of the importance to "win the minds of the people", investing a part time of an expensive professional into that educational capacity, possibly aiming to explore Agile frameworks other than Scrum, building the awareness, and laying the foundation for a deeper cultural change;

2. In a hybrid rather than dedicated Agile Coaching role situation that we are looking at in this hypothetical example, the expectations of the Leadership would likely include you planning and facilitating some training sessions on Agile Fundamentals and possibly beyond;

3. This won't be just your classic SM role with basic set of responsibilities that we've listed above but will expect you pushing above and beyond the basic Scrum delivery cycle level. You'd better have the moves and knowledge to back it all up if deciding to proceed with your job application.

So the most important thing to note here and be aware of is that applying for an SM/Agile Coach role you'll be expected to demonstrate a lot more maturity and proficiency in Leadership and coaching skills than any interviewer would expect from a straight up classic Scrum Master.

Make sure you can substantiate your claims of such experience - if you decided to go for this role regardless - with practical examples of turning things around, professionally convincing stakeholders that Agile methodology is better suited to achieve their goals.

Be ready to prove that you've trained groups of people in a structured and methodical way, organized and facilitated 1:1 and group coaching sessions, Team-building activities, knowledge refresher exercises, investing a lot of time into establishment of a sustainable Continuous Improvement culture.

Agile Coaching is a deviation from the core Scrum Master role, not a direct evolution.

Because it's primary purpose shifts from optimizing Product Delivery within the scale of one (or a few) Scrum Teams, into driving adoption of the Agile Mindset and assisting with the positive cultural change across the whole organization.

As with the other Agile hybrid roles being advertised on the job search websites, you'd do well to confirm as much as possible in terms of the actual expectations of your potential employer, their plans for the future, such as possibly impending large-scale Agile Transformation they are building up Agile Coaching muscle for.

Obtaining Relevant Experience

Repeating what I've told you already – having relevant work experience *or finding a way to convert your experience into something that appears relevant* is one absolutely non-negotiable requirement for you to get hired as a Scrum Master.

We won't talk here about the obvious exceptions of someone simply being in the right place at the right time, and the luck turning in their favor where their employers was giving away promotions and Scrum Master titles as part of a larger scale transformation, simply because they were too cheap to get qualified people from the open market.

In that case you wouldn't need anything more than an expression of interest where you appear enthusiastic and likeable enough to immediately score a goal and get the job most of the readers of this book want.

Let's return to our case where you are applying for an advertised Scrum Master role as an external job seeker, with no magic fairy godmother who would be able to help you bypass many requirements and jump over the competition.

We'll also need to assume that you haven't been working as a Scrum Master or Iteration Manager before, as otherwise the subtopic of how to make sure you appear as a person with relevant work experience would become irrelevant to you.

Good news is that a lot of professional activities other than acting in Scrum Master capacity could be considered relevant and have some conversion value when you present that experience correctly in your application for the Scrum Master role.

If you have at least a couple of years of working as a team leader of any kind, especially in Digital Production or Software Development, or have been exposed to Software Development Lifecycle, gathering and documenting Business requirements, or Project Management, you'd be in a reasonable position to present that experience favorably enough in your CV to not be discarded as a SM job applicant immediately.

As I've mentioned already, I'll do my best to give you the general gist of what you should be looking for when trying to follow a Do-It-Yourself route, but when your career pivoting situation is not trivial, considering to employ an Agile career coach could be a better option.

I can't speak for every recruiter or hiring manager out there, but I know that a lot of people including myself believe that hiring people for Agile roles is more about spotting the right personality and attitude, supported by demonstration of the basic skill and ability to handle team dynamics of general nature.

As some tag lines say: *"Hire for attitude, train for skill"*.

Being realistically prepared for what the job market would throw at you in terms of competition and requirements is the first step to overcome the potential fear and anxiety when trying to assess your own chances of getting through that initial filter.

Your success as a less qualified applicant with no direct prior Scrum Master experience depends on the clean and clear presentation of your achievements and professional persona, and luck.

I'll mention luck as a factor we shouldn't shy away from acknowledging further in the book, but in this context I'd be lying if I told you that you don't need to be somewhat lucky to be called by the recruiter and get through to the interview as someone who stretched their CV, rephrased their prior experience to make it more appealing and showed some form of appealing personality in their Professional Profile.

While you explore the ways to obtain that relevant experience or rephrase and present your existing one into something of interest to someone looking for a Scrum Master, let's not forget the obvious need for you to understand the Scrum Framework very well.

You will lead with that knowledge and even basic Scrum Master certification in your CV in any case, as that is an expected baseline for any successful applicant.

If you've only been a Software Engineer or a Tester, were you exposed to Agile or Scrum process at all?

If you have in fact been part of the Development team following Scrum delivery method, things are looking up for you already. Scrum teams frequently use the rotation of Scrum Master "hat" as the opportunity to develop their people and encourage further ownership of the Scrum process.

You'd have to decide for yourself how much you'd be willing to stretch the truth without becoming unethical in your application if you know that you have the moves and you're familiar with Scrum process enough to perhaps say that you were "acting" Scrum Master in the past.

This would effectively look like you've had relevant experience, suddenly sky-rocketing your chances of being seriously considered for this Scrum Master position, compared to where you'd have been without it.

As a person who interviewed a lot of job applicants not even being a professional recruiter, I will admit that I also wouldn't trust unsupported claims that someone could perform particular duties while nothing proves that they've actually "been in the trenches", gaining experience that's very different from a picture-perfect classroom Scrum Master training.

This leaves us with one tough question that I'll do my best to address below.

No Experience – Now What?

I think making sure you have realistic expectations about your chances being employed as a Scrum Master is very important, as it saves you the time banging your head against the wall, armed with only positive attitude and hoping to get lucky.

There's nothing wrong with trying or staying positive and confident in your personal abilities. But if somebody stops you and suggests - *"Take a break and apply for another transitional role, that doesn't come with such steep entry level requirement"* - you'd have overall higher chances of getting where you want to be, actually gaining some proper experience along the way.

So if you don't have any prior Scrum Master experience, and don't belong to one of the professional categories we'll discuss in the chapter about transitioning from different applicable roles, you really only have the following options:

1. **Trying to look for a lateral move within your current company**, where you'd get a magical promotion if they suddenly need Scrum Masters but can't be bothered looking for talent outside their organization.

More realistically however, your Manager could perhaps give you an opportunity to shadow a current Scrum Master, maybe even allowing you to perform their duties as some form of a voluntary extension of your current responsibilities.

This would give you a sense of really being a Scrum Master in the field, providing learnings you can't get from training courses, until you experience those yourself;

2. Work with an Agile Career Coach or try and **consider the Scrum Master role as a step after** a role that you might need to take right now, to bring yourself closer to your goal and gain some relevant experience along the way.

I personally found moving into Agile Business Analysis much easier than effectively managing delivery of digital value as a Scrum Master or Iteration Manager. Business Analysis requires analytical mind and exposure to requirements gathering and decomposition into Backlog items.

Practice shows that convincing the employers that you are able to do that is easier – and a lot more reliant on the applicant's positive personality and other traits where they work well with people – than one's ability to suddenly start acting as a Scrum Master without evident prior experience.

This option also includes Internships and Graduate Programs that you'd have to research in your area, where Google becomes your best friend. You'd expect to meet qualifying criteria to be employed on the lowest possible salary or as "free help" (definitely not common in Australia but possibly used somewhere in the United States) to do what's required around the office and get exposure to an Agile-based software development process.

Having some of that experience to put towards an application for a Software Engineer or a Business Analyst position in a properly Agile environment would set you off on the right path towards becoming a Scrum Master.

3. **Not recommended**, but to be fair in listing all of the available options that work for some people – you could, basically, lie.

Rewriting your CV where your prior experience is presented in a way that brings forward your agile attitude, teamwork, exposure to Scrum Framework through your own learnings, how you've always promoted team collaboration, business involvement in decision-making, and the other elements of the new ways of working is something that I'd call an *ethical stretch*.

In fact, I'd go as far as saying that a lot of people wouldn't have been in their new jobs these days if they haven't done some form or level of that ethical stretch. At some point all of us need to go beyond our current comfort zone, or active duties to take on something new. If only the people who have always done something exactly like that before were given certain roles, there would never be fresh blood in those positions.

Lying however is something of a different scale and level, in my opinion.

It is when someone clearly hasn't performed any of the duties they claim to have had and done in the past, basically making things up and hoping that the illusion will hold long enough for them to get the job they want, and fake their activity in it long enough until they become part of the furniture, or decide to move on somewhere else.

Sad thing is that I've spoken to several people who have anonymously confessed to have used this very dangerous approach that eventually worked for them. Some literally lied their way into the job that wasn't technically hard enough to perform without any prior experience, later becoming everyone's friend and therefore not being critiqued or watched closely enough to call out discrepancies in the claims made on their CV or their actual performance.

I've also heard about a few cases where the bluff was called and the professional image crash that the person experienced was horrific enough for them to move cities and eventually find a job elsewhere, as the local job market was narrow enough for the word to spread pretty fast.

Regardless, everyone decides for themselves how desperate they are to get a job without having the right experience and not willing to take middle-steps to gain that experience somehow before taking the leap straight to their goal.

I'm not here to judge your personal circumstances, so I'll stick to listing the options you have.

But did I mention clearly enough that I don't recommend this method?

Value of a Scrum Master Certification

Technically speaking, you do not need a Scrum Master certification of any kind in order to start performing duties of a Scrum Master. But whether or not you'll be seen as a worthy job applicant without a certification while every other applicant has one, is a different question.

Scrum is a free framework, with clear-as-day and widely known Scrum Guide that you could download, read at your leisure and apply the learnings at your workplace immediately - given the opportunity provided by your employer, or the Program of work.

Usefulness of certifications emerges when you need to breach that virtual wall of recruiters or any other hiring process that looks at you as an unknown entity. Remember that those people don't really know anything about you, where you came from, what work you've done in the past and to what standard?

Certifications have always been a method to tell the world that you've really dedicated your time and resources to a certain subject matter, as well as proven your certain level of knowledge to a respected panel of judges, or a certain authority, that effectively gave you a "stamp of approval" in the form of a piece of paper you could put up on a wall.

Scrum is not the most difficult thing in the world to master, and most Agile frameworks aren't either, until you get into the depths of Scaled Agile implementations within large corporate organizations, or face really difficult circumstances asking for creative pivoting and falling back on the knowledge that doesn't come from any place other than real world experience.

Scrum Master certifications however became an acceptable method to state your readiness to take on SM responsibilities, making you a better candidate in the eyes of almost any recruiter or hiring company.

Always remember that in the abundance of choice of the job applicants, you will be inevitably compared to someone who is likely to have a relevant Agile credential, or a lot of experience in the field of Agile Delivery.

I see a growing trend in the modern recruitment process surrounding most Agile Delivery roles including Scrum Master ones, where just showing your fancy certification badge is no longer enough to pass through the filter of the interview process, even if you've managed to get past the initial screening process done by the external recruiter.

That is once again mainly due to a large number of qualified professionals on the market, who can show both the Scrum Master certification, and support it by practical real world experience delivering Digital Products, coaching the teams, and bringing real value to other businesses they used to work for.

In some less common cases similar to my own, someone could get a Scrum Master or Iteration Manager job mainly relying on the experience and clear examples of previously delivered Products and contributions they've done to recognizable companies, with zero to very little reliance on a supporting piece of paper with three letters on it.

There's another trend to bring to your attention here:

Most recruiters who deal with the hiring of the Agile professionals are well aware that many larger companies often send their own Project Managers and other staff on Scrum Master courses, therefore granting them a Certified Scrum Master (CSM) certification "by default", whether they really wanted and worked for it, or not.

It then becomes a really meaningless label from both the perspective of an employer, and the employee.

So a lot of hiring people understand that Scrum Master certifications -- especially the de-facto industry standard CSM -- sadly became a bit of a tick-box in too many cases these days, requiring strong evidence supporting your factual Agile work experience, or another respectable Scrum Master certification, like Professional Scrum Master (PSM) from Scrum.org.

To summarize all of the above, Scrum certifications are valuable, and can definitely help you, if you have anything to back those up with. I don't believe that they count for much as a standalone achievement.

And because we are talking about maximizing your chances of being hired in any way available to us, I'd conclude that you should get at least one relevant Agile Scrum certification, like PSM, even before you decide to invest into something more expensive, like CSM.

Professional Scrum Master Certification authority - Scrum.org - allows you to prepare, read their guide, and take their free Open Exam, to test your basic knowledge. Trouble with that Open Exam is that it has not much in common with the real thing you'll face when trying to sit the actual exam for your PSM 1 certification.

You'll see an odd question from the Open Exam during the real test, and it will stand out like a good friend you haven't seen in ages, but it won't help you much as they give you 80 much tougher questions to answer, with a global ticking timer allowing about 2 minutes for each answer.

I've seen guides that help you prepare for PSM exam, and this book is not one of them. So you could choose your own preparation path here, but I encourage properly experiencing Agile Delivery environment (in a different role perhaps), and learn Scrum Guide back to front as the solid starting point before attempting the exam.

Scrum Alliance organization was there first, and their Certified Scrum Master (CSM) is more widely accepted as a Certification that will get you past the initial recruitment screening process - subject to the trend I've described above, where CSM specifically is often prompting extra set of interview questions from a recruiter or hiring manager.

CSM is also considerably more expensive compared to PSM, and in my opinion doesn't necessarily test any specific knowledge that PSM exam doesn't take a good swing at.

I see more companies hiring Scrum Masters listing both CSM and PSM as optional advantages to all applicants, which I think demonstrates a lot more mature and fair recruitment process that one could engage in.

Finally, if you believe that the more certifications the merrier, you may want to consider taking on our own Lean-Agile Certified Practitioner exam you can find at JoinAgile.com and add that to your wall of achievements that might tip the scales of the job candidate selection process in your favor.

Since we mentioned our LACP certification it would be only fair to elaborate that our exam is aimed at senior Lean-Agile practitioners, validating their knowledge well beyond Scrum Framework, into Lean Kanban and realistic team dynamics scenarios.

You might want to keep it in mind for your future Agile conquests, after you've obtained your first Scrum Master title and have performed the role for a few years.

Basics of Job Transitioning

As a professional who decided to leave their current role or even industry behind and become a Scrum Master, you realistically wouldn't just start applying for Agile Delivery roles, if you want to have any chances of success, that is.

You'd have to undergo a phase of professional pivoting, readjustment. You'd try and gain insights and a perspective upon the different job market, filling in any knowledge gaps, obtaining the new relevant experience and updating your CV accordingly first.

I refer to this phase as *"Transitioning"*, which should hopefully sound self-explanatory.

When you decide to transition from your current job to another one, you should ask yourself the following closely related questions:

1. How far am I from my goal right now? Am I able to assess the size of the actual gap between my current role, skillset, the industry and the desirable target state of joining Agile Digital Delivery process in some company as a fresh Scrum Master?

2. How do I capitalize on my existing skills, and use my existing knowledge and experience to the maximum potential during this job transition? What can I reuse as a relevant asset, when applying for the new role?

In this chapter we will take a closer look at the most common job transitioning cases, from the roles that would arguably offer the most logical and less tricky path to eventually receiving that Scrum Master job offer.

Software Engineer or Tester to Scrum Master

Software Engineers are most commonly referred to as "Developers", at least in Australia. So when I mention developers please keep in mind that the terms mean the same thing and will be used throughout the book interchangeably.

Developer to Scrum Master job transition is fairly common, yet might not be the easiest or smoothest journey compared to some other combinations we'll talk about below. This type of transition sometimes requires an extra transitional "middle-step" that I've mentioned as one of your career pivoting options in the previous chapter.

If you've been a Software Engineer or Tester of a team operating under some form of Agile Operating Model, then the step forward to becoming a Scrum Master would be very logical and easier for you.

In this case you were likely exposed to the Agile ways of working, the language, principles and some practices that your existing Scrum Master, Iteration Manager or Agile Coach might have involved you in.

You would have surely worked or at least heard of the User Stories, Product Backlog, Agile Board and the authority of the Product Owner to make calls on what's most important for the team to work on next.

You would have also then had a chance to observe your current Scrum Master or another Agile champion in action. If you're anything like me during my career transitioning years, you would have then been paying attention to what they do and how, perhaps even taking notes on how certain events and ceremonies were run.

Taking this hypothetical scenario one step forward and assuming that Scrum process you've witnessed or been directly exposed to was more mature, you might have even seen the attempts of your Agile champion of the area to empower Software Engineers such as yourself to take ownership of certain processes, letting you be in the driver's seat.

This would effectively allow you to feel and claim that you've acted Scrum Master on several occasions, which would make your updated CV look a lot more attractive to the potential employer who is looking at you not as the Developer anymore, but as someone who pitches themselves as a competent Scrum Master.

Not everything relies solely on your exposure to Agile principles and practices however.

Scrum Master role requires slightly different personality than your typical Software Engineer is believed to have. Scrum Masters must have demonstrable desire to work with people, talking and explaining things to them on a daily basis, being extraverted rather than introverted individuals.

While this trait is expected a lot more openly from a role such as the Product Owner or an Agile Business Analyst, Software Engineers are known to be relatively quiet types, *who like to code and be left alone*.

This stigma-based and slightly "tunnel-visioned" statement comes from the understandable fact that in general this is the case with Developers. Exceptions to this general rule however are not unheard of, with yours truly being one of those introverts at one point in my early career.

We are who we are, but setting the right career transitioning goals would lead you towards realization that you'd need to consciously work on developing what we call *adaptive behaviors* in the coaching practice. Put simply, it means that you see the greater good for yourself from progressing towards your desirable new job, at the expense of training yourself to put on a social mask, get out of your comfortable behavior zone and play a role your new job requires.

A lot of people would tell you – be yourself, never compromise – and all that nice-on-paper stuff. I won't.

Because I understand the complexity of job market, career progression and difference between my personal life preferences versus the satisfaction my job gives me. In other words, I might be an introvert who gets reenergized alone, but I still get satisfaction from helping people adopting the new ways of working or changing their careers towards agility.

So I had to adapt and learn how to fit into the shoes of a Scrum Master, Delivery Lead, and a coach, because the good from the satisfaction that my job now gives me is much higher than the initial struggle I had creating that "work personality" that's not necessarily hundred percent aligned with who I am on the inside.

I didn't jump straight into the Scrum Master or Iteration Manager role because I lacked thorough understanding of Scrum process – beyond the theory of the Scrum Guide – and felt like the job market back then was more friendly towards Engineers who sought Agile Business Analyst roles.

So I picked that middle-step, got the job after a couple of months of focused searching, and learned a lot about Product Backlogs, requirements elicitation, User Stories and the Acceptance Criteria along the way.

I truly believe that the middle-step I took made my transitioning journey smoother and resulted in me being a much better educated and all-rounded Scrum Master and Iteration Manager.

This story I've shared with you doesn't mean that you have to take the same long path of transitioning via Business Analyst role like I did.

As we've discussed in the previous chapters, with some luck and specific circumstances where you've been a technical leader or subject-matter expert of the team, facilitating technical meetings or knowledge-sharing brownbag sessions, you could present that experience as very relevant and somewhat similar to what any employer would effectively expect their Scrum Master to do.

Add a demonstration of your motivation and passion for the new ways of working, a new Scrum Master certification and knowledge of Scrum Framework, and you'd have decent chances to looking just as good if not better than the other Scrum Master job applicants – especially if a particular job ad highlights very hands-on and technical environment where you'd fit right in!

Career transitioning is all about finding the ways of presenting your strengths in a way that fits into the role you're seeking.

Let's quickly look at those that a typical Software Engineer would possess and could capitalize on in their rewritten CV and during the potential job interview:

1. You would have an understand of the end-to-end Software Development Lifecycle (SDLC), including the phases of scoping, development, testing, and digital product deployment.

This knowledge should be put to the forefront of your newly written *"Technical Scrum Master"* CV that you'd use to apply for job ads that are clearly stating how important it is that you have a good understanding of how development teams work. Trust me, those highlights are frequent in the job ads, if you're paying attention or know what to look for.

If you had any exposure to DevOps ways of working, I'd say you will be among the job applicants with the highest chances of being taken seriously by the employer and taken into the face-to-face interview phase at the very least;

2. As already mentioned, you would have been an active part of a real development team, collaborating with your colleagues, solving technical problems together, and possibly even presenting the fruits of your labor to the End-users or the Business of your organization;

3. You could hopefully claim that you've had exposure to Scrum Framework and Agile principles by the virtue of being part of an Agile team, under the supervision of your Scrum Master. This is a specific point where you might want to revisit the previous chapter where we talked about how far would you be willing to stretch the CV and truth about your actual responsibilities, without hurting anybody or jeopardizing your professional ethics.

Have you been given a chance to act as a Scrum Master, or would you be willing to say that you have, because once or twice you had to facilitate team meetings and Scrum ceremonies when your Scrum Master got sick? It is up to you to determine that fine line, staying on the side of this dilemma that would allow you to remain comfortable with how you'd be pitching yourself for the role.

If you claim to have certain abilities or experience, be bulletproof about your ability to perform at that level. We all stretch when we want to reach higher. The point is not to break your back or fall down embarrassingly in the process!

Needless to repeat that you'd have much higher chances of being considered for a Scrum Master position if your CV says that you've been acting Scrum Master, rather than saying that all that you've done was coding and testing software, and that's it…;

These are just a few solid hooks that you as a Software Engineer or

Tester who is willing to try and position themselves as a Scrum Master could hang your hat on, at least initially.

With your prior experience being properly presented on your freshly rewritten CV you won't look as useless as someone who felt like they have literally nothing to offer the employer work experience-wise, and solely relied on their personality and a freshly obtained Scrum Master certification.

Business Analyst to Scrum Master

Let's start by making sure that our personal understanding and definitions of the Business Analyst (BA) roles align.

When I say "BA", I talk about a person serving as a conduit between the "Business" and the Scrum Team.

The term Business usually encompasses the areas of your organization who deal with the Customer. They are non-technical, and typically aren't expected to understand how the sausage is made. But they know really well what types of sausages the Customer likes, how many they consume and by what date they'd like a certain type of sausages delivered.

Business Analyst then works with the Business representatives to understand and dissect the requirements they have for the new types of sausages, including all the desirable ingredients, without going into the detail about how those sausages will be made or what would ensure that the Scrum Team produces the required quality and quantity of sausages as quickly and sustainably as possible.

Are you still following my simple analogy here? I think it works quite well!

Business Analysts have existed for as long as the Project delivery had existed, utilizing variety of traditional and more recently Agile methods of capturing and tracking the Business requirements.

To keep the content of this book relevant to the main topic and not deviate too far off course, I'll be mainly talking about an Agile-savvy Business Analysts. Those who understand what a Product Backlog, Epics and User Stories are.

Agile Business Analysts typically work as "proxy Product Owners" in the larger Agile programs of work where the Business struggled to supply sufficient amount of the empowered shot-callers who could be embedded within the teams.

This shortage of the actual Product Owners is rather common in the Australian corporate landscape, almost always creating a demand for the helping hands of an Agile Business Analyst who could amplify and propagate the efforts of an already stretched actual Product Owner.

With all this being said, an Agile Business Analyst would be among the easiest roles to transition towards a full-time Scrum Master occupation, and here is why:

1. Working as an Agile Business Analyst you would have to be exposed to the Agile value delivery process of some kind. The chances of you being at the very center of Scrum process that someone else was perhaps facilitating are very high;

2. A lot of companies I've personally worked for and spoken to are employing a hybrid role of a BA/SM, mentioned in one of the chapters above. So if you were one of those, now trying to transition into a full-time Scrum Master position, it should be a piece of cake for you, with a few minor tweaks of your CV and a little luck.

If you weren't one of those hybrids, looking to apply for such a hybrid role could be a very smart first step towards becoming a full-time Scrum Master shortly after, for all the obvious reasons;

3. Business Analysts are likely to have the right personality to become a good Scrum Master.

BAs are working with people, and usually know how to deliver their points across, as well as being good at hearing people out. As a Scrum Master you focus more on the people and the process, rather than the requirements or the Backlog Items that you would have been polishing up to this point.

So the core communication and collaboration strengths you'd possess as a good BA would be very transferrable into the world of Scrum mastery, with a little shift of your focus that you'd have to demonstrate to your recruiter and potential employer.

But what if you are **not** an Agile Business Analyst and only had experience working with the Excel spreadsheets, long Requirements Definition Documents and Traceability Matrices?

Then you should guess that I'd recommend an extra and potentially shorter middle-step for you on your journey to becoming a Scrum Master by first seeking involvement in the Agile Product delivery, and learning about Agile Business Analysis as a layer on top of your traditional BA skills and experience.

You would largely follow the same approach as I've recommended for Software Engineers and Testers, where you'd try to highlight your experience and skills that have conversion value for the Agile ways of doing things.

This could include your experience running requirements gathering workshops, assisting with Project discovery sessions, any forms of staff training or knowledge sharing. Any people-centered activities where you've been driving certain process forward and collaborating with the development teams and stakeholders would be of direct and high conversion value for the new ways of working and Scrum mastery specifically.

Your experience analyzing and dissecting work, preparing digestible technical implementation instructions in the form of Business requirements of some sort is still directly translatable to the new format of the Agile User Stories. You'd just have to learn more about the Product Backlog and practice writing good User Stories, to feel more confident with the teams that are already consuming Business requirements in that format already.

Applicable to professionals transitioning from any role that had zero exposure to Agile Delivery process before - not just Business Analysts - my advice will remain generally the same.

You need to seek the opportunities to partake in that Agile Delivery process, either by joining up with the Teams practicing those processes and requiring you to play the same game for a while, or by establishing such a process of your own, within the professional area and responsibilities that you have some control of.

Project Manager to Scrum Master

Traditional Project Managers (PM) are the people of control, in its most classic "Command and Control" form.

They strive to define every piece of the puzzle upfront and know where each of those pieces is at any point of time, how long will it take to complete each of these pieces of work, and if the whole operation is still fitting into their precisely scheduled project budget.

Project Managers are detailed planners, and the fans of Abraham Lincoln who suggested to spend a lot more time sharpening the axe before chopping the trees down. Please forgive a loosely reworded quote, but it delivers the right message regardless.

PMs are trained over the years to be this way in order to stay efficient and get the projects over the delivery line. That's all they do and caring about Delivery Team members involved in that process, or relinquishing even part of that overall control would be one of the last things coming to a traditional Project Manager's mind.

Scrum Masters view and approach things very differently.

First of all, they understand that they don't directly control anything. Instead, they encourage and facilitate the empowerment of the Scrum Team members to take control over their commitments, quality and the whole delivery process.

Being in a project delivery role too, Scrum Masters also need to know where the things are at, and if there are any risks or impediments that their Team is experiencing that they might need help resolving.

Usually the Scrum Masters or Iteration Managers still need to keep a close eye on the "Story Points burn", having conversations and providing team performance reports to the Project or Program Managers supporting their Scrum team. Scrum Masters need to be on top of what the team is doing to guide the process until the developers take charge and embrace the Agile mindset, assisting with facilitation of ceremonies, and the more involved Scrum processes such as the Sprint planning and estimation of the User Stories.

So the Scrum Masters also control things, but indirectly.

They promote the value delivery process where the team would be encouraged to take a few swings at that metaphorical tree, and then inspecting the axe to check if it requires further sharpening or slight adjustment of the angle to ensure that the chopping process keeps going smoothly...

Now I've feel like I've taken that Abraham Lincoln quote as far as one ever could!

Scrum is about transparency, inspection, evaluation, and adaptation of Team's approach during the further Product delivery stages, rather than having an End-to-End plan most Project Managers are conditioned to love and require upfront in a non-negotiable way.

All in all, in my personal opinion, transitioning from being a Project Manager to becoming a Scrum Master would be the hardest career pivot to execute.

Your core mindset and approach would be the furthest away from where you'd need to be to look and act the right way to convince the hiring management that you are the best candidate for the advertised role.

Having said all of the above and being brutally honest with you as always, this job transition is certainly not impossible.

Everyone is different, and of course one could work at changing their viewpoint, retraining themselves to see and approach things from a different angle. As you've figured out by now, I personally believe that the PM mindset and the default approach they'd take in project delivery would be the biggest hindrance to them becoming a good Scrum Master.

As we did reviewing the other roles, let's list the recommendations I could give a Project Manager to start changing their self-presentation towards something a lot more Agile-friendly, and develop a persona that could be potentially considered for a Scrum Master role.

1. Look around and see if you are in – or close to – an Agile project delivery environment, where you have Scrum Masters working on your projects, perhaps providing you with the Burn-down charts that you've needed to produce your financial forecasts, projections and project plans so far;

2. While normally not a recommended practice, you could request an invite as a silent observer into some of the Scrum Team's ceremonies. This would allow you to learn more about how Scrum Guide theory applies to the real life processes in the project delivery trenches.

This would be immensely helpful for you to further visualize yourself in the new role of a Scrum Master, or maybe even conclude that this Agile world and mode of operation is not right for you;

3. Be transparent with your Delivery Teams about your aspiration to be closer to the Agile culture and Scrum practices, talking to your Scrum Masters and Agile Coach if you have one in your area.

Request an opportunity to shadow a Scrum Master or facilitate some of the ceremonies for the team, once you feel like you've got a better understanding of how those should be conducted and what their purpose really is. Best way to learn is by doing something, and this ground rule almost never changes;

4. Ask an Agile specialist, coach or a recruiter to review your current CV and provide suggestions on how you should rewrite it.

This advice generally applies to any professional willing to pivot their career, and is only emphasized here for completeness of the chapter and the fact that a traditional PM might require extra assistance to look "more Agile" on paper.

Other Roles to Scrum Master

I believe enough context was already given about the attitude, personality, skill-set outline, and the general professional outlook required from anyone who wishes to transition from their current role to being a Scrum Master.

We've already reviewed the roles that I believe represent the vast majority of those that have realistic chances of transitioning towards Scrum Mastery, with some revision of their skills and prior experience, or by planning an extra middle-step for their career before they achieve their end-goal.

This is not to say that the other professionals, such as Project Coordinators, Coaches, Trainers, Teachers cannot set a goal to become Scrum Masters and succeed at it.

All I'm suggesting here is that for those "outsiders" the path towards Scrum Mastery will likely require more than one middle-step and potentially a lot of extra and specific self-education.

To become a Scrum Master or get hired for another role that's close to your target, such as Agile Business Analyst, you'd first need to find an entry point into the industry and the professional space of Agile Project Management and Digital Delivery.

You could be a people-person and a successful team leader of construction site workers, suddenly deciding to become a Scrum Master, and I'll tell you here and now – don't let anyone stop you, go ahead, just hear me out first.

Regardless of your possibly impressive previous experience and however many people you've worked with in the past, you would benefit personally and professionally from trying out the waters of our industry first, by considering one of those roles more suitable for your eventual transition to that of a Scrum Master.

It would almost certainly mean undergoing some Information Technology / Digital training, attending courses and obtaining relevant certifications. Realistically, you'd be aiming to first arrive in one of the roles that were described at the top of this chapter as the most suitable for Scrum Master transitioning.

This path would likely require your readiness to accept the roles more junior than your current one, expecting a pay-cut, but benefiting in the long run from being exposed to the world of Software Development and Digital Delivery, seeing what the Agile champions and Scrum Masters specifically are doing day by day.

Look at your experience and personal preferences and decide what would be the "bridging solution" that suits you best?

Are you interested in Software Development or Testing? There are plenty of courses and online materials that would allow you to pick a niche such as Front-End Development and dig into it, learning HTML and one of the more popular frameworks such as Angular JS, React JS or Bootstrap.

Or maybe project management path would be more suited for you?

Then you'd most definitely have to learn a lot about the methods of project delivery in the modern day and age, obtaining relevant qualifications before you'd try and apply for one of those roles, bringing you closer to where you'd like to be in the end.

Importance of a Great CV

Understanding what to expect from being in a Scrum Master role and knowing what is likely to be expected from you is important, which is why we've spent a sizable amount of time going over a whole lot of points that have hopefully helped you better assess your readiness to go ahead and apply for one of those Scrum Master jobs advertised on LinkedIn or anywhere else today.

Now it's time for us to start talking about the actual artifacts and methods that will help you get over the hiring line.

First, we'll cover a good Agile Resume (or CV), as the most important element of your personal pitch when applying for any job on the market. Then we'll move on to discussing your Cover Letter as something that is frequently overlooked as a critical element of any effective personal pitch for the new role.

While you can't get far without certain personality and knowing the subject matter relevant to the job you're applying for, the first point of your interaction with the recruiter or the potential employer will always be your CV and Cover Letter, if you bothered to write one.

You've basically shot those two documents into the dark and now sit there hoping to hear something back.

The one goal of this book is to increase your chances of getting a response to your application, and proceeding past this virtual barrier towards the further stages of the hiring process.

The response we all hope to receive as job applicants is an invitation for an interview, and that's what we'd be striving for. But I'd like you to consider and understand that these days in the oversaturated job market of 2020 it is very common for many applicants to never hear back from the recruiters, which is the worst case scenario that we'll try and avoid at all costs.

Hearing back from the recruiter or the hiring company with some form of feedback other than a *"You've been unsuccessful, better luck next time!"* default bounce-back email, should be seen as a good thing.

Better recruiters and employers would bother speaking with you and commenting on your experience or how you've chosen to present yourself on your CV, which is valuable information you should always pay attention to and see as an opportunity to adjust your self-presentation slightly, if it means reasonable increase of your chances to be successful next time.

The way this CV reception and bounce-back process is handled varies greatly depending on the external middlemen recruiters, or the actual HR department of the hiring company who might be handling your job application directly.

While there are no hard and fast rules following which would guarantee success to your job applications, there are some established and solid patterns that I'll share with you here and in the further chapters that should increase your chances of at least proceeding to the next stage of speaking to the hiring management face-to-face at an interview.

Whether the recruitment process is handled by an external recruiter or internal HR department, the methods of CV handling and initial job applicant screening are varied and evolving every day.

Understanding the goals of the talent acquisition personnel better would help us devise a strategy of improving your CV. So what do those people really want, as middle-men of the hiring process?

These people primarily strive to create a shortlist of job applicants that match the job description and requirements most accurately. Nobody wants to spend more time than absolutely required to do a certain task, and the time-poor recruiters are not an exception.

In some cases, and abundance of the received CVs, the recruiters priorities looking at those rather than reading your Cover Letter.

Under other circumstances, where the cultural fit of the candidate is most important to their Client, or when they've been sorting through the applicants and not finding anyone their Client would like, they'd start paying attention to extra personal detail, such as the pitch you'd embed in your Cover Letter – we'll talk about it in the next chapter.

Assuming that the CV screening process is performed manually and not with the help of some fancy A.I. powered system, behavior of which would be almost impossible to predict in this book, the talent acquisition person would most likely pay attention to the following key points:

1. Does the applicant's CV contain their professional title, and does this title match the one on the job description?

2. How clean and readable is the applicant's CV?

3. Does it contain the keywords that the Job Description they've received from their Client highlights as mandatory skills and qualifications?

4. Does the CV show the last three to five years of relevant experience?

5. Does the CV mention any big or famous company names where the applicant worked in the past?

This list is certainly not exhaustive, but should give you an idea that a human reviewer would always optimize their time when looking at potentially hundreds of CVs to quickly get a snapshot of your professional persona.

They are triaging your case very quickly against the others and deciding if it's worth spending more of their time calling you on the phone to check how you sound, and seriously considering then to add you to their shortlist of people to interview.

And hopefully it is also clear by this point in the book that regardless of who is reading through your CV and the Cover Letter – both should be rock-solid and utilized effectively to maximize your chances of going past this initial barrier that so many job applicants are failing to breach.

The 15 Seconds Rule

Expanding on the sentiments made above, and now clearly understanding that optimization and clarity of your self-presentation is key when preparing your CV for your new Scrum Master role application, it is good to know about the *"15 seconds rule"*.

It is believed that an average recruiter spends about 10-15 seconds to size up a freshly received job applicant's CV. That is still assuming they are using a real person to scan the received Resumes, and not relying on a fully automated and A.I. powered system that would make our preparatory guesswork here even harder…

The good news is that regardless of the employed CV ingestion and scanning method, at some point a real person would have to take at least a quick glance at your CV, following the recommendations of the filtering A.I., or simply looking through the hundreds of emails in their Inbox.

At that point your CV needs to be very well laid out, cleanly formatted and easy to read, allowing that person to get a clear picture of you as the best candidate for the job, who puts forward most relevant information and has nothing to hide.

Using my prior experience as an example here once again, I've been involved in the process of reading through received job candidate CVs many times, shortlisting those who got my attention for a face-to-face Interview.

My involvement in this on-boarding process was rather late in the presumable chain of events that the job applicant had to go through before I even got to see their Resume sent to me by the external recruiter.

That particular external recruiter must have filtered up through dozens more, before actually sending some of those CVs to the hiring management that I was assisting with the Agile Transformation at that time.

Once the CVs reached my desk for review, I didn't use any of the automated candidate competency testing methods such as the one we currently offer at JoinAgile.com, or any of those crude keyword searching patterns that should have told me if the applicant mentioned a certain Agile framework enough times on their CV.

Instead I've actually spent time reading through the candidate's personal profile, if they've included one on their CVs, and quickly glanced over what the applicant included on the first page.

I don't know if I've actually spent 15 or the whole 30 seconds to pass my initial judgment, but overall I can confirm that whoever is looking at your Resume would unlikely spend more time to read through every line of your included professional experience to figure out who they are dealing with here.

This is one of the most common misconceptions among the job seekers I'm coaching these days, that even if they don't bother to summarize the information about themselves on the first page of their CV, the recruiter will bother to read and comprehend the rest of their CV.

I can confidently tell you that this assumption is false.

While I do pay attention to how cleanly laid out the CV is overall, as that tells me about how organized and neat the person is in real life, when pushed for time to review dozens of CVs I too won't spend my time to dig out the gems that you might have had in your past.

If you didn't bother presenting those pearls of your professional past to me in an easily digestible and accessible manner, why would you expect me to do that excavation work for you?

It is only fair to add here that those implicit requirements for clean and tidy CV that is structured a certain and rather simple way will depend on the actual role you are applying for.

Presentation of a CV belonging to an organized Project Manager or Scrum Master would be certainly different to the Resume of a designer from some creative agency.

During the time of my Agile coaching and transformation leadership I've reviewed hundreds of CVs and all of them had something to do with Agile professional space, which I suppose puts a certain lens over all of my comments in this book.

But with that in mind, the book is teaching you how to become a Scrum Master or prepare for another role that's close to our space, so I guess my comments would still broadly apply for the topics we are discussing.

But a lot of people claim that "CV is dead"…

As a wrap-up to this chapter I'd have to add this little segment specific to the late 2019 and early 2020. Many LinkedIn influencers have indeed made claims that the traditional *"CV is dead"*, and that it's basically replaced these days by your LinkedIn profile.

Being the author of this book that deals directly with the best ways to present yourself as a great job candidate to the potential employers, I couldn't just finish editing my book without expressing my own opinion about these claims.

Put simply, I think those are largely attention-seeking and personal brand-promoting outbursts that are not substantiated by any prominent enough trend or movement for majority of the recruitment firms and individual professionals I've spoken to.

Online presence, including your public profile, publications, achievements, references and possibly even the trail of your employment history becomes more and more prolific these days, without a doubt.

LinkedIn became THE professional social network that has no equal in the early 2020, and is a hub of job ads and personal social postings from both the job seekers and employers.

And while many companies require you to provide the link to your LinkedIn profile as part of their job applications these days, I'm yet to see one that says *"your LinkedIn profile is sufficient, don't worry about attaching your CV..."* They still want to see both, as those employers perfectly understand that the society hasn't moved on in its behavioral patterns far enough yet to discard the traditional elements of presenting yourself professionally to someone else.

The industry of business cards suffered from the presence of online profiles much more than our CVs, as we in fact see fewer and fewer instances of someone offering you a physical business card these days when you meet them.

But LinkedIn profiles are nowhere near replacing traditional CV fully, and probably won't be for the next five years at the very least.

We need to always remember that we deal with human behaviors and not just technology that enables those behaviors. Online profiles are not as strong an invention that would suddenly make you stop using cars and start flying with your new jetpack, because it's clearly so much more convenient that everyone started using it immediately!

Humans are creatures of habit, and habits are even more prominent among more traditional organizations, such as government structures and well-established financial institutions.

So if you're in doubt, I'd like to clearly recommend to you to put your efforts into creating a solid CV that you use to apply for Scrum Master roles, and also maintain a similarly phrased and certainly not contradicting LinkedIn profile.

It will be looked at by many recruiters and should not clash with whatever the personal image you are trying to produce on your CV as you transition your career towards Scrum Mastery.

Attributes of a Good Scrum Master CV

Regardless of what the overall layout of template you've decided to use for your CV, it's the content that matters the most. You need to tell the most important and relevant things quickly, before you've lost the recruiter's attention.

We've already discussed at high level that the content needs to appear neat, relevant, not mixed up with qualifications and experience that has nothing to do with the job you're applying for, and easy to navigate so that the reader can find all the necessary information.

Let's highlight the most important guiding principles when planning the structure and content of your CV:

1. **Your CV is not your biography**. Nobody cares about literally everything you've done in the past. Only the information and qualifications relevant for the job should be presented to the recruiter.

2. Your CV needs to effectively **answer all the questions** that the hiring manager asked their applicants to address in the Job Description.

3. Related to the point above – many think that the more different proficiencies, interests, qualifications and achievements you list on your CV, the better. In the modern over-saturated job market this assumption is false. People mostly look for **more narrowly specialized** people who would do a particular job well.

4. **Do not use a one-size-fits-all CV** for all of your job applications, unless you are only applying for the exact same type of a Scrum Master job advertisement. This is where the same CV should pass fine, and you'd only need to tailor your Cover Letter a little bit, but we'll talk

about those points in the next chapter.

Now let's dive deeper into the already mentioned elements of a good CV, and discuss how exactly you could make those happen in your instance.

Clean Presentation

There are so many CV templates you could find right now without spending a cent and within a couple of minutes time, provided you have access to the Internet.

Google Docs is one example of a completely free platform that would offer you dozens of templates to choose from and make the use of. My recommendation is for you to not try and be original or fancy, and pick a nice, simply laid out template with a clean header, neat and readable headers, supporting bullet-point lists and tables.

Steer clear of colorful templates with curvy frames or any imagery. Scrum Mastery is a form of Digital Project Management, so you need to come across neat and organized, not particularly creative.

Keeping it Short

Some free Resume writing guides will also give you this basic advice, but tell you to try and fit it all on a single page. I've been there myself and know just as well as you do that it's virtually impossible, if you want to bring any useful information across and unless you are straight out of University with zero work experience.

But in that case I've already mentioned that you shouldn't be trying to get a Scrum Master job, and would do much better planning your more modest middle-steps on your career journey.

My recommendation would be to try and trim your work experience to only the most relevant information that highlights activities and achievements that a Scrum Master would be involved in, keeping it all on three pages, maximum four.

As you should have figured by now, you need to make the first page count.

It doesn't mean overloading it with information like a densely packed newspaper page, but to be pickier about what you put on it and in what order. We will discuss this particular point in more detail very soon.

Limit the work experience to the jobs you've had in the past 5 years, and wrap the section up with a statement that the details of the earlier roles are available upon request. This usually satisfies 99% of recruiters and hiring management.

Do not use "one size fit all" CV

As already mentioned, a one-size-fits-all CV would only work if you are only applying for one specific job type and title, such as the Scrum Master positions.

But if you have a generic *"Scrum Master / Iteration Manager / Business Analyst"* CV that you throw at every Agile job you can find on the market, I guarantee that it'll look sloppy in the eyes of the recruiter or

HR person sorting out the job applications, with yours landing in the bin pretty quickly.

Use the same job title as the job ad or description asked for. If it's an Iteration Manager job ad, do not apply with a "Scrum Master" CV.

I know that your responsibilities would likely be identical and it appears very pedantic, but you can't assume that the junior 20-year-old recruiter newbie on the other end of the line would figure out that those mean the same thing, increasing the chances of them preferring CVs of those people who told them exactly what they hoped to see.

Additionally, when the recruiter asks for a specific industry or domain knowledge experience – *Financial Services, for example* – make sure to highlight clearly if you've worked in that industry and what your achievements have been there. This point will be even more relevant when preparing your Cover Letter, as it allows for a slightly more free-flowing and tailored narrative than just stating your previous job titles and responsibilities in your CV.

Do not overthink this element where you'll start doubting yourself and feeling like you're writing too close to what the recruiter must want to hear, as in vast majority of cases this is exactly what they hope to receive from you, and you could always clarify the specifics that you've put on your CV when somebody calls you for a chat.

Personal Profile Section

I'll just say it how I see it here – you should always start your CV with a short but clear Personal Profile section. It serves as a quick professional summary of your persona, your recent achievements relevant to this job, your passion and aspirations.

It is debatable if the recruiters would skip it or read it, but I know I pay particular attention to this section and many of my colleagues do to. This is my way to see if you can describe yourself well and if this description hits the right notes as far as I'm concerned, when trying to pick the right person for a job.

Having said that, I probably wouldn't discard a CV without a Personal Profile, then paying particular attention to where the person worked for in the past and have there been enough details provided about those previous roles. But why reduce your chances to produce a great upfront impression?

Hence my recommendation that you should definitely bother to write one, and make it good.

As Scrum Mastery and Agile Transformations become more and more common to many professionals on the job market of 2020, these professional concepts became demystified over the past few years.

Many recruiters and hiring managers now understand that being a great Scrum Master or Agile champion who will help promote the new ways of working is a lot about personality and demonstrable activity that the person might have had, even if they appear to have less years looking after the Scrum Teams compared to someone else.

I personally hire for attitude and motivation, not for the years of experience. A lot of people I've spoken to share this view as well.

So for you writing a good Personal Profile could be one golden ticket to meet the interview panel face to face, where they'd certainly dive deeper into your experiences and qualifications.

Don't forget the purpose of your CV – it does not replace your self-presentation during the interview. Nobody expects to read your CV and "have no further questions". All your CV needs to do is to spark enough interest and confidence in the recruiter or hiring manager so that they decide to spend more time talking to you, that's it!

Education and Qualifications

I suggest that you neatly format your highest education degrees and relevant qualifications as a list of bullet points or a table, and put it straight after your Personal Profile.

This quickly tells the employer about your academic achievements if any, which for better or for worse adds to the picture of your persona that you've started painting for them, and how far have you taken your career in terms of Agile-specific qualifications.

From the perspective of your qualifications that would likely make your CV passable in the eyes of the recruiter, you should at least have one Scrum Master certification – **PSM** or **CSM**.

I'm personally not a fan of long lists of every certification imaginable, as this could backfire on the applicant presenting them as a "credential collector", while not really proving anything to the potential employer about how well you'll be able to get along with everyone.

But some baseline Agile qualification is required without a doubt, and I'd seek to obtain one before trying to apply for any Scrum Master roles.

Summary of Key Skills

I recommend that you follow your list of qualifications with another list or a neat table of your key skills you'd like to present to the potential employer.

This part is critical, as while the hiring manager would be without a doubt more interested in your personality and overall tone, the middle-man recruiter or HR person will be still ticking boxes of your skills versus what their Client asked for in their Job Description.

As with the work experience, there is a noticeable tendency among the less experienced job seekers to dump every imaginable skill they have into this section, often making it very bloated and unreadable. Don't do that.

Read the job description and requirements to make sure you aren't missing anything in relation to what would be expected from a typical Scrum Master or Iteration Manager in any organization.

Make sure you mention what's relevant, not everything you might have done or got good at over the past 20 years in the coal mining industry where you've perhaps started your career. I hope you're getting my gist here.

I've personally reviewed job applications of people applying for an Iteration Manager role position with a completely unedited original 10 years old CV of a traditional Project Manager. They didn't mention one word about Agile or Scrum, or the new ways of working. Their Key Skills were PMBOK, PRINCE 2, and *"Management of large programs of work on time and on budget"*.

I'm not even joking; I wish I was!

Key Skills I'd hope to see among yours when you apply for a Scrum Master job – *not necessarily word for word!* – would include:

1. Scrum Framework – Agile theory and Scrum implementations in small-to-medium sized companies;

2. Efficient facilitation of workshops and team-level ceremonies;

3. Full SDLC, working as part of Software Delivery teams;

4. Project-level reporting – Burn-down charts, Product Roadmaps, and more;

5. Team collaboration tools – Atlassian JIRA, ServiceNOW, Microsoft Teams.

These list entries certainly don't hard-limit everything that a Scrum Master could be potentially exposed to or responsible for, but set a healthy range of what your average Scrum Master job opening would be aiming to cover with their new recruit.

Employment History

Some recruitment consultants recommend including Key Achievements into the segment listing your Employment History.

I recognize that Achievements are important for a lot of jobs that have easily quantifiable KPIs or responsibilities, such as the Project Managers.

Their CVs are full of *"Delivered Program of work X that saved $20M for the company…"* entries as achievements preceding the more commonly expected bullet points listing their actual responsibilities in that previous role.

Scrum Master responsibilities are different, which is often reflected in their CVs. It's a welcome sight to see something similar to the line quoted above in a Scrum Master CV, as they might have been with a particular Scrum Team that was responsible for launching some awesome new Product that the new hiring manager might have heard of and would be impressed by.

For example, I've interviewed an Iteration Manager job applicant recently who has given us a very clear example of their proudest moment being the launch of Digital Driver's License Mobile App for the Australian Roads and Traffic Authority. It was an impressive achievement that was worthy of a mention on their CV without a doubt!

But when it comes to more commonly expected project delivery budgets and numbers saved for the company that we are used to seeing on the traditional CVs, we wouldn't get many of those when dealing with Scrum Masters.

These examples lead me to my point that you should assess your personal situation and decide if listing some particular achievements would improve the overall look of your CV, or would it just bloat it with information where your contribution would look too vague?

This choice is very much up to you and your personal circumstances. Yet again I'd have to mention that if you have access to a career coach, you should expect them to be able to look at your personal achievements closely and tell you if those are worth including in your Scrum Master CV or not.

The meat and potatoes of this section is the Employment History itself.

It should be presented as a sequence of clearly laid out segments consisting of the title you had back then, the name of the company, duration of your employment including months and years, and a reasonably short list of bullet points telling the reviewer about your main responsibilities.

Your employment history segments should be ordered in a descending order, with the most relevant and recent experience at the top.

One question that I get asked very commonly is how short is too short of a work experience that would not be worth including on your CV, to prevent an impression of you jumping around from job to job too often?

The answer is sadly depending on your individual situation yet again, and would be seen as right or wrong very subjectively. I'd say that generally you should attempt to group up any short-term work experience with duration of less than 6 months into one batch rather than listing those as individual "jobs" as it looks easier on the eye of the hiring manager.

I'd also say that in the present day and age shorter term contract engagements are very common, and not many companies would frown upon someone who hasn't had a job lasting for longer than a year over the past five years. Some people simply work on contract engagements because it allows them explore the industry better, and the contracts get cut left and right, which has nothing to do with their ability to stay in one place over longer periods of time.

On the flip side of that coin, some people could come across very "institutionalized" if their CV says that they've stayed in the same job for over 10 years. This could come across short-sighted and judgmental, but this is the reality of our industry and fairly young new ways of working movement.

If you didn't feel the need to explore the job market, learn about how different companies implement Agile and specifically Scrum practices, mellowing behind the thick walls as a Tester or a Software Engineer for over 10 years, I'd personally think that you're not nimble, motivated and responsive enough to be one of my Scrum Masters. And many people would feel the same.

The point here is that when you plan your career and are still far off your retirement years, you need to recognize the need to "keep the heartbeat up", move around the industry, seek exposure to different companies and ways of working.

All of this adds to your professional value and this will be surely seen by a better educated and modern employer.

Hobbies and Interests

Mentioned here only for completeness purposes, and because I keep seeing a lot of my colleagues and job candidates I've interviewed who decide to include this information in their Resumes.

I'll keep it simple and tell you that you should leave it out of your CV. I keep it out of mine, and never read one if a job applicant decided to include it.

If they are interesting enough to invite to a face-to-face interview, we'll likely discuss their personal interests and hobbies, but there is no reason to include that in your professional pitch.

Having said that, you need to pay close attention to how the job ad is formatted, as there could be significant presence of how much your potential employer invests into their Team sports, family culture and similar things.

It is quite rare to see, but certainly a welcome sight among generally bland bullet-points of what they expect their Scrum Master to do.

So, if you've noticed that a particular Agile job ad you are responding to gives a lot of weight to, say, Team soccer, then suddenly your hobby of playing Soccer on the weekend becomes a lot more relevant than before and worthy of an honourable mention!

Scrum Master CV Template

We've discussed the general rules of laying out a good Scrum Master CV, what content elements should be included and in what order.

Unfortunately, the format of an eBook and difference in page rendering that different readers offer these days doesn't allow me to simply include one neatly presented Scrum Master CV template in here.

I will however attempt to put what we've discussed in the previous chapter together into the resemblance of a template below, that you could use as a vague guideline when formatting your own.

Pick a clean CV template in Microsoft Word or Google Docs, paste or type in the sample lines that I offer you below, and then tweak and change according to what actually applies to your own case, keeping things as real as possible and not stretching the truth about your prior achievements too much.

Also hopefully needless to say that the template below is kept brief, incomplete, and only giving you an outline of the employment history segments that you'd then copy and paste as many times as you need to, reflecting your last 5 years of work.

Without any further ado, let's give it a shot:

JOHN SMITH, SCRUM MASTER

PERSONAL PROFILE

Certified Scrum Master with over 5 years of experience in Software Development and Digital Product Delivery in Financial Services and Telecommunications industries.

Passionate about the Agile ways of working, empowering people, and continuous improvement. Great influencer and motivator with the proven record of successful project delivery and fostering a high-performing team culture.

EDUCATION

University of Technology (UTS), Sydney, Australia

QUALIFICATIONS

- Bachelor of Technology, UTS, Australia
- Certified Scrum Master (CSM)
- Professional Scrum Master (PSM 1)

KEY SKILLS

- Agile Frameworks - Scrum, Kanban;
- Agile collaboration tools – Atlassian JIRA, Trello;
- Coaching and mentoring of the team members;

- Technical Team Leadership;

- Stakeholder management of different levels;

- Front-end development background.

EMPLOYMENT HISTORY

Jan 2018 – Present | Big Australian Bank, Sydney

Key Achievements

- Scrum Master and Agile Coach for the teams that delivered $2M award-winning Project X in 2018.

Key Responsibilities

- Facilitation of Scrum ceremonies, including Sprint planning, Daily Scrum, Sprint Reviews, Retrospectives;

- Assisting the Product Owner with Backlog refinement and teaching them how to write better User Stories;

- Reporting to the parent Program on the burn-down rate of the Scrum Team;

- Part of the Agile Community of Practice, collaborating with other Scrum Masters on the best methods and practices helping us introduce positive Agile culture.

What this quick example would have hopefully demonstrated to you is that the most important information has to always go first, and we need to be rather ruthless in trimming any of the potentially plentiful but irrelevant facts about yourself that the recruiter wouldn't be interested in.

It is always a balancing act between trimming too much information to keep only relevant items, and ending up with a rather barren CV. I trust you to use your common sense and imagination here a little bit to land somewhere in the healthy middle, without swaying too much towards one or another extreme.

Make it easy for the recruiter and the hiring manager to find the right information about you, silently answering the question of why should they see you as one of the best candidates for this particular role and interview you face-to-face?

If you get a good feeling when asking yourself this question after editing and reading through your CV yet again, then the chances are that you'd be in a good spot to proceed to the further points that we'll discuss in the following chapters of this book.

Writing a Cover Letter

What is the purpose of any Cover Letter, and is it still important to prepare one?

Although the times have changed and the focus of the recruiters has shifted towards the CVs a lot, Cover Letters are still considered good form when applying for a job, or even expected by some of the more traditionally inclined organizations.

Those more traditionally trained recruiters, HR personnel and hiring management still pay attention to your Cover Letter, reading it first and then deciding if they should spend more time to review your certainly more information-packed CV.

Cover Letter is a shortcut for the hiring manager to get to know you better without meeting you in person or digging through the bullet points on your CV. A well written letter could make or break your employment, and I've been employed in the past on two occasions mainly thanks to my Cover Letter, as I was later told by my bosses at that time.

Having said that, I wouldn't dare presenting myself as a Cover Letter writing expert.

I'm only here to tell you that those are still important and shouldn't be skipped in 2020, when the job application process allows you to attach one to your form, rather than skip it. If the employer uses their own specific job application submission system that doesn't ask for it, or won't allow you to attach multiple files to your application – so be it.

But where you could use this little leg-up on others who haven't bothered to write one, you should definitely capitalize on the opportunity and spend a few minutes composing a Cover Letter.

My recommendation follows the basic rule of thumb I've been preaching to you throughout this whole book – capitalize on any opportunity to present yourself to the potential employer as well as you can, not cutting corners or skipping steps that might reduce your chances of getting hired.

It is important to understand that your Cover Letter is not just a trimmed repeat of what you've written in the Personal Profile section of your Resume. While your Profile talks about you as a high-level summary of where you're at with your career and aspirations, Cover Letter is an opportunity for pitching yourself for this particular role in a lot more personal and targeted manner.

While your CV needs to be tailored for the job you're applying for, it often remains unchanged in many areas such as your employment history if you keep applying for similar Scrum Master job ads.

Your Cover Letter however should change every time, more explicitly talking about why you've applied for this role, and why you'd be a great fit.

Here you would expand on your past achievements that you believe would make you look as a more attractive Scrum Master role candidate, and politely ask for an opportunity to present yourself to the hiring manager in person.

These are the implicit rules of the game and the steps of a fancy dance we all have to play to match the mental picture of a great, forthcoming and motivated employee. I recommend that you stick to this pattern in 2020, until we have reasons to believe that these generic expectations started changing across the Agile job market.

In the Cover Letter you should aim to respond to every question that the employer or recruiter representing them has asked in the job ad.

For instance, if the job ad says *"Financial experience is highly desirable"* and you don't have any, you might choose to address it head on in your

Cover Letter by saying something along the lines of *"While I haven't worked in the Financial Services industry in the past, I've performed similar duties while working for a travel company, and believe that at the end of the day my job as an Agile champion is to empower the people, enabling their collaboration and productivity by introducing the methods and principles that are industry-agnostic."*

Your wording doesn't have to be as fancy as that of course, but the message would tell the hiring manager receiving your application that you've seen their requirement, didn't ignore it, and addressed it with something that shows you as a mature Agile practitioner who understands the important elements of your role, versus simply ticking the box of having worked for a bank or an insurance company before.

From the Cover Letter template perspective, it's the same as with your CV – there are plenty of free and professionally laid out templates available in Microsoft Word, Google Docs and from the other sources.

Just pick and use one, don't overthink it.

I recommend saving both the Cover Letter and your CV in PDF format which will ensure readability and in some cases will prevent ingestion into the employers automated systems, prompting for a review by a human being.

As far as the extra Cover Letter pointers are concerned, don't forget to date and address it appropriately. It's a "letter" after all.

Most job ads in Australia mention the name of the contact person within the company, or the recruiter who is effectively the one receiving your application. The rule of thumb here is simple – make your Cover Letter as personal as possible, addressing the recruiter by their first name, where their first name is known.

Saying *"Dear Ian..."* is always setting a friendlier tone, than a generic *"Dear Sir or Madam..."* would do.

As with your CV, I recommend that you keep the language of your Cover Letter very clear, professional, and easy to understand. You want to list the relevant information and make your point, without pouring too much water into your text.

In addition to keeping content of your Cover Letter simple and to-the-point, professional recruiters recommend using plain and readable fonts like Arial 11pt, where there is no need to get any fancier than that.

Don't forget to include your own name and contact details – *email address and mobile phone number would do* – to make sure your Cover Letter can be matched with your CV in the rare cases of their system storing both documents separately.

Begin your Cover Letter with a clear and confident statement about why are you applying for this role, and why think you'd be a good match for it.

Then add a brief paragraph telling the recruiter about your most recent and relevant experience that further explains how you think you could be of use to the employer's organization, reinforcing the message of why you are a great candidate.

You could mention your years of experience working in a certain environment, or implementing Scrum framework elsewhere, for example.

You could optionally expand into how excited you are about the possibility to work for their company and why, but keep in mind that while a lot of companies say that *"people are their main asset"* and all that, they still have a profiting agenda in mind, where fulfilment of their needs with the person who will get this job comes first.

Soft sentiments that stroke the ego of the hiring manager and tell them why you'd love to work for their awesome company are great, if they are used sparingly and as a small addition to the bulk of content that speaks about what they are interested in the most – why they should potentially give this role to you.

The last paragraph should wrap up the Cover Letter, expressing your desire to meet the recruiter or the hiring manager, depending on who you are addressing, if that chance presents itself.

Desire to meet the team, see what their current culture is like before formally joining the ranks is usually seen as a very positive quality in a job applicant almost without exceptions.

So your angle when presenting yourself to the recruiters and employers via your Cover Letter and the CV should always be about what you can do for them first, and about what their organization can do for you second.

Cover Letter Template

Same as with your CV, I'd expect you to find a nice and clean professionally laid out Cover Letter template, and use the following indicative content as the filler that would help you express your own thoughts when applying for any Scrum Master job.

Attn. Chris Brown

Recruitment Company, Pty Ltd

Monday, 18 December 2017

Dear Chris,

I've seen your advertisement for a Scrum Master position on "JobSearchWebsite.com", and decided to apply as I believe my skills and experience would be perfectly suited for this role.

I'm currently working for the "Big Australian Bank" as an Agile Business Analyst, and acting Scrum Master.

I look after two Scrum Teams and work on the Product Backlog refinement, helping the Product Owner write better User Stories and create the Product Roadmap. At the same time, I'm involved in daily Scrum team activities, facilitating Scrum ceremonies and being the first point of contact for any impediments that require resolution and can't be dealt with by the team itself.

I'd like to use this opportunity and take on a full-time Scrum Master role, as this is where I'd like to take my career in the future. I believe my good knowledge of Scrum Framework and process, as well as experience of working on the Product Backlog and Business requirements elicitation would be a welcome combination of skills for your respected Client.

I look forward to hearing back from you, and would love an opportunity to introduce myself in person at your earliest convenience.

Thank you,

John Smith

0408 111 000

johnsmith@someemail.com

As you can see, I've included a quick summary about the job applicant in the Cover Letter, why they would like to work for the company offering the job, how their skills are relevant and what's in it for the Client that the recruiter is representing.

With any luck, these 3-4 paragraphs of text would give the reader an impression of the applicant being a skilled and motivated professional, who knows what they are doing and where they are headed professionally.

This image would without a doubt increase the chances of this applicant getting through to the next stage of the hiring process, which might be a quick screening phone call from the recruiter, followed by the face-to-face interview.

Company Research

Most of the experienced job seekers would confirm that doing the research of the company offering the job could dramatically increase your overall success chances of getting hired.

While those findings might be hard to reflect in your CV or the Cover Letter, you'd without a doubt benefit from demonstrating some knowledge of the company vision, culture, or the latest publicly known achievements during the face-to-face interview.

In this chapter we'll talk about when you should conduct your research, and what methods you could utilize to find out as much as possible about your potential future employer.

When I talk about Company research, we could virtually subdivide this process into two types – *specific* and *non-specific*.

You'd need to do non-specific company research when you are brand new to Agile Project Management and Digital Delivery professional space, and simply want to find out what companies offer the jobs of that kind.

What companies are hiring Scrum Masters and other Agile champions? Are any of those located in your area? Do you prefer large corporate entities, or smaller start-ups?

These are only a few of the questions you'd likely have in mind when starting your non-specific Agile-hiring company research.

You'd obviously need to start looking closer and digging deeper into the profile and Internet footprint of a particular company when applying for a specific job.

As already mentioned, the insights will potentially help you make your

Cover Letter appear more informed when explaining why did you decide to join them and apply for the role, or even augment your CV further by bringing forward certain experience and achievements that would resonate better with the hiring management.

Even more common reason to do specific company research would be as part of preparation of your Resume and Cover Letter, smartly tailoring your self-presentation to what is likely to match hiring company's internal culture and other expectations.

One point that we haven't discussed for a while is that while generic job requirements for a Scrum Master are fairly consistent on the job market, the companies are known to put their own extra spin on the role.

And this would be one of the key elements and pieces of information you'd try and fish out from the Internet or by using LinkedIn to reach out to someone who might have worked for this company in the past.

Starting your research as early as possible will dramatically improve your chances at almost every stage of your application process, from tailoring your Cover Letter before actually applying for the role, to the final rounds of face-to-face Interviews with the hiring managers of the company.

What Information to look for?

In short, any information about the company and roles similar to the one you are aiming to perform there – Scrum Master in our case – that doesn't come from any sources interested in "selling" you the job.

Let's not forget that even helpful recruiters are interested in selling yourself as a type of Product to their Client, the hiring company with a vacancy for a Scrum Master.

So if they couldn't find the candidate with the right cultural fit factor, or skills, or any other qualities that their Client is looking for, they'd suddenly become the second most interested party in finding you a job and trying to present a particular opportunity as a chance of your lifetime.

It's a double-edged sword, really.

As you most certainly want them to see you as a hot commodity and the best choice of an employee for their Client, but at the same time you need to be very aware of the "interested party" element when asking your recruiter for any insights about the company.

This is not to say you shouldn't always try and ask your recruiter questions like *"Do you know how the culture is at this company actually? What's the employee retention like? Do they mostly hire permanents or contractors?"* And so on.

Recruiters often give you some helpful information about the company and often even lead with it, rather than wait for you to ask them, but there will be a large dose of deniability in what they tell you about the company culture and how happy are people they know inside the company.

This is not the only reason why you should always do your own and independent research, that's as unbiased or utilizing as many sources of information as possible.

Because even if you find someone on LinkedIn who reveals some organizational horrors to you that should turn you off that company because they've personally had problems with some manager in there, it doesn't mean that it will be all bad for you.

Any insights should be taken with a grain of salt and cross-checked wherever possible.

Having said all of the above, I'm not suggesting that you turn your job search and interview preparation into an episode of Sherlock Holmes TV show. Try and find out as much as you can because usually this will help you in one way or another. But don't turn yourself into a detective as there's a law of diminishing returns that applies to the research process, just like any other.

Don't overdo or become obsessed with it.

What information are we looking for, specifically?

I'd divide the types of information you'd be looking for into these two often intersecting groups:

Public Information:

This would contain any openly shared information about the services and Digital Products that the company is producing, their organizational structure, any known goals or Vision, and their Mission Statement perhaps.

Geographic locations of their offices hiring Scrum Masters and the other "Agile people" are also important, as it would make little sense aiming to work for an employer who located on the other side of the country, when you have zero desire to relocate.

Insider Information:

Obtaining these insights is understandably harder, but not impossible. If any information would have the potential of making you double your efforts in preparing for the interview and trying to get this job, or turning you off applying altogether – it's this type, most certainly.

Usually these insights would come from someone you could talk to directly, in person or via LinkedIn messaging, and who used to work at the company, now willing to share what their experience was like on the inside.

You'd typically start by asking about or searching for the information on the company culture, how they treat their employees, career advancement opportunities, particular bosses if you know the names of the hiring managers, ballpark salary ranges, and similar things that are shared less commonly in the open social media feeds.

How to do your research?

There are plenty of methods to do your research, starting from obvious ones like reading through the sections of company's website and their newsletters you can locate, and finishing with something that requires a bit more effort and personal networking efforts.

I'll list a few easily accessible research methods below, as I find them very effective when used at the right time, and with the clarity of purpose in mind - as you always should pick the right tools for the right job.

"Best Agile company" search

This method would be of highest benefit to those job seekers who are brand new to the industry and Agile Project Delivery professional area, you could run a few Google search queries for *"Best Agile companies in Sydney"*, or *"Agile consultancies in Austin, TX"*.

This research option would most certainly unearth a lot of website links and LinkedIn mentions of what we'd commonly refer to as *Agile agencies, or consultancies* that have spawned in great numbers over the course of 2018-2019.

These companies do not do any Agile Product development themselves, but instead seek to acquire a pool of qualified Agile resources – mainly Agile Coaches, Scrum Masters and Product Owners – and then subcontract those to their sometimes broad networks of Client companies.

In my opinion, getting employed by one of these "Agile agencies" would be among your highest chances of getting hired as a fresh and career transitioning Scrum Master, who is looking for work on the open market, rather than being promoted internally.

This is not to say that these companies aren't picky when it comes to who to hire in 2020, quite the opposite.

Keep in mind that when you talk to non-specialist recruiters or hiring managers who aren't specializing in Agile methods and principles, your conversation with them becomes a lot easier during the interview.

In other words, those people would be less likely to pull you up on some inaccuracy in how you've described running a certain Scrum ceremony to them, and throw less curve-ball questions at you like *"What should a Scrum Master do if the Product Owner got sick and became unavailable to their Scrum team for a few weeks?"*

Agile agencies however are established and ran by the Agile practitioners, who know their trade very well and are usually trying to differentiate their services from the other similar agencies by trying to attract as much top-tier Agile talent as possible. So they would most certainly apply a lot more critical and probing view to your CV and verbal answers during an interview, if you get invited to attend one.

So why do I say that it's one of your easiest employment options then?

Purely because of the numbers of vacancies that those companies would have open, versus some actual corporations and software development houses that seek to hire a Scrum Master directly.

Some Agile agencies are simply on the constant lookout for "good people", so if you look reasonably attractive as a potential consultant on your CV, the chances are high that they'd at least want to take a look at you face-to-face during an interview.

Searching for Scrum Master jobs

Going on your local job search website and running searches for Scrum Master jobs would be the bread and butter part of your research, always.

If you are really clueless to where people look for jobs these days, as you've been deep underground in a mine somewhere in the middle of Australia for the last 10 years now deciding to become a Scrum Master – *yes, I'm being a little sarcastic here, forgive me* – you could always ask your friends what job search engine they are using these days.

I've listed this research option second, because we aren't talking about job search per-se in this chapter, and are still focusing on finding out more about the companies offering Scrum Master roles, rather than aiming to jump straight to applying for jobs.

Also, the job ads are often posted by the external recruiters who would not reveal the name of the actual hiring company until they've screened your CV and decided to talk to you about the actual role and who their Client is.

This limits the insights gathering element of this method substantially.

When you see the names of the companies openly posted in the job ads, or once you've managed to get past the first hurdle of getting through to the recruiter and having the initial meet-and-greet chat with them in person or over the phone, you'd be able to proceed with your company research, knowing who those people are.

LinkedIn lookup

LinkedIn network became a lot more prominent in the field of job advertising, rather than just networking and profile listing.

So you could do both the Agile job search on LinkedIn these days, as well as looking up the company name and then spending some time reading the content they've been sharing over the past few months.

You could find different articles, shout-outs, job advertisements they might have reposted directly in their social feed. If you take this research seriously, observing what kind of content is the company posting, liking, supporting in any other visible way could tell you a lot about the culture and vision in action, rather than just relying on whatever they wrote on their website.

All this however would still be mainly in the "Public Information" category, so what you'd really want to do is try and find profiles of people who are either currently working at this company, or have worked for them in the recent past.

You goal would be to find people working for this company in a Scrum Master or any other Agile Delivery role. Attempt to get in touch with them by sending them a connection request or direct message if they've allowed it in their privacy options.

I'd then politely introduce myself and explain that you are considering to apply for a Scrum Master job with this company, asking for any advice or insights that the person would be willing to share, perhaps over a coffee.

There are obviously no guarantees that the people would honestly share any valuable insights with you or agree to meet you, so be prepared for no response whatsoever, or something that would be far from helpful. Take it for what it is – you are trying all options, and if you don't try, you won't get anywhere. So it's usually worth a shot.

I have to stress here that reaching out to someone and asking for some insights or a chance to pick their brain over a coffee is very different from spamming them with messages if they didn't respond to you, or stalking them in any other way.

Know the limits of this research method and don't become a nuisance.

GlassDoor.com research

Less widely known or obvious but probably one of the most effective methods to obtain some "insider information" about the company you'd like to work for is by spending some time on *Glassdoor.com* or the regional version of this site, such as *GlassDoor.com.au* for the Australian job market.

Glassdoor is a job and company information search engine, that's not guaranteed to have the insights you are looking for, but it's certainly among the best services out there that would expose information that you'd struggle to find anywhere else.

Their database used to mainly contain anonymous company reviews and salary insights that were really useful even back in 2016 when I've published the first edition of this book, but now Glassdoor evolved beyond that point, apparently giving you options to search for job postings, do your company research and compare salaries.

I'd definitely recommend that you visit and explore Glassdoor when doing your research, or even just looking for Scrum Master jobs. An extra job search engine and a source of potentially valuable information has never hurt anyone.

Regardless of the company research method you choose, information is your ultimate power, and perhaps that extra little edge that's required for you to stand above your competition in the overall recruitment process.

Additional good news is that researching information on a particular company also increases your overall knowledge of the industry and professional space of Agile and Digital Delivery. So the next time when you are reading about a potentially similar company hiring a Scrum Master, your previously researched company could end up being their primary competitor.

Being able to demonstrate great knowledge of the industry the hiring company operates in, including their competitors, is one of the things that could help you stand out during a face-to-face interview.

And this is definitely the positive effect you want.

Preparing for the Interview

After doing all the hard work of researching the Agile Delivery employment opportunities in the industry of your choosing, preparing your CV and applying for a few jobs, you will eventually get to the point of preparing yourself for the face-to-face interview.

Getting through the recruitment filter, making sure your Cover Letter and CV stand out enough to be noticed can be a challenge, but the actual interview with the hiring managers of the company offering the job will be what's going to count at the end of the day.

So let's make sure you are as prepared as possible, and have very realistic expectations of what kind of personality, behavioral traits, and knowledge a Scrum Master needs to demonstrate to the interview panel in most cases.

Job interview process usually starts with you meeting the recruiter first, and then proceeding to the second round of meeting with the representatives of the employing company. Sometimes this process involves additional steps like having to pass an online test that would help your perspective employed gauge your professional Agile competency level and behavioral traits.

JoinAgile.com offers one of those easily accessible systems that is now trailed by the few Australian recruitment companies, and it is not the only candidate screening system on the market that was built to help make the interviewing and hiring decisions more educated.

This is basically to tell you that the interview processes and the steps involved vary greatly from company to company and are impossible to cover or 100% prepare for in advance, without knowing what specific job you're going for, and where.

One element of the interview process that generally does not change, is the part where you sit down with usually more than one person from the company you'd like to work for, and have to tell them about yourself, answering specific questions they'd have prepared for you.

The rest of this chapter is dedicated to those questions that many employers would be likely to ask you. Spending some time preparing answers to these questions would mean less stress on the day when you're forced to think on the spot.

Don't forget that the interview panel doesn't just want to hear your answers to specific questions. They also observe how you deliver those answers, do they come naturally do you, or are you stressed and appearing caught off-guard all the time.

Needless to say that preparation is the main method to reduce your interview anxiety, letting you breathe and appear friendly and present in the room, naturally creating a much more appealing image of yourself as someone these people might need to work with in future.

"Tell Us a Bit About Yourself"

I'd bet significant amount of money on this question being among the first two you'll be asked at most interviews. The importance of starting the conversation smoothly and being prepared for this part, making your answer sound as natural and free-flowing as possible to set the tone of the interview right can't be understated.

The most important part to understand here is that nobody is interested in your whole life story and the question doesn't mean *"tell us everything about yourself"*.

The interviewers are looking for a brief summary of your personal and professional background, with specific focus usually being placed on what you've been doing at your last place of employment.

But don't just tell them about how you ran Scrum ceremonies and talked to the Business stakeholders about the importance of Scrum process. While this could be a part of your narrative – *you're applying for a Scrum Master role after all* – my point here is that you should try and weave in some information about who you are, and why you became a Scrum Master.

Again, this doesn't have to be a long story, but I've always enjoyed talking to the interviewees who came across human, rather than just spitting out exact and one-two line answers to the questions I've asked. Remember that the people interviewing you are looking for someone who they'll be working with and who will be around their people all the time, not some fine-tuned machine!

Try and prepare a speech that fits into one or two minutes.

Rehearsal at home when you're speaking out loud rather than just read through your notes over and over is key and will significantly improve the way you sound and come across.

"Why do you want to work here?"

This question could also come in a form of *"What was your reason for applying?"*

You should this as an opportunity to demonstrate your personality, and the depth of research you've done on the company. You could compare your personal goals and beliefs with the vision of the hiring organization, highlighting how working for them as a Scrum Master would satisfy your professional aspirations and personal preferences.

I love asking this question during the interview as it often tells me everything I need to know about the job candidate, often as far as allowing me to make my preliminary judgment on whether or not I'd like to work with this person.

You have to be aware that when you're interviewed by senior professionals or hiring managers, they would have interviewed and worked with many people over the years and can sense your tone, personality and cultural fit pretty quickly.

This is not to say that if you weren't able to sound as smoothly or aligned to the mood of the people in the room perfectly, you'd have lost your chances of being hired. Far from it. There would most likely be plenty of follow-up behavioral and technical questions where you'd have a chance to add to your picture of a great potential hire. I myself have been in many situations where initially bland-looking job candidate came out of their shell some ten minutes into the conversation after they've warmed up a little, and ended up getting the job.

When talking about yourself, remember that the hiring panel is mainly interested in your professional achievements of the recent path in the area of Agile and Scrum Mastery specifically.

Yes, I've just told you that framing all that in a nice and very personable presentation is very important, but they are still hiring someone who needs to appear proficient in delivery of digital products and looking after Scrum Teams. Do not lose sight of that fact.

"Why should we hire you?"

This question could be phrased softer, and sound something like *"What would the people who know you say makes you special?"*

Answering the "why hire you" version can be usually handled shorter and pointier, and the key gist of your response should be – because you believe that you are the best person for the job.

How you'd choose to articulate that without sounding arrogant is up to you, which makes preparation and practice of what your response comes across as most important. What you tell the interviewers in response to this question will also depend on how much you already told them about why you'd like to work there.

While when you told the interview panel about your interest in their organization you might have spoken already about how you believe your skills and professional aspirations align with the values and direction of their company, in this question you'd do well to single out a couple of personal traits that would give you extra flavor in their eyes, or add some extra value to your persona.

I'm not suggesting that you should reuse any of the responses I'm about to offer you below, but these should help you generate some ideas of what you could say about yourself:

1. *"Because I offer unique combination of skills, not just the knowledge of Scrum Framework..."*

2. *"Because I'm naturally inclined to take personal accountability for the performance of the teams I'm looking after..."*

3. *"Because my prior engineering experience would put me in a unique position of being able to speak the language of developers, rather than approach everything purely from the Scrum process perspective, not understanding the reality of what the developers are going through."*

When preparing and rehearsing your answers, the best way to shock-proof those is to ask yourself *"Am I actually coming across as the best person for this job?"*

"Maybe not" might be an acceptable answer, but only inside your own head and while you still have time to adjust your self-presentation and prepare for your interview pitch better.

It's easy to forget that the interview process is usually a game with only one winner. It's not enough to end up in the top three of their job applicants. You need to progressively build your persona in their eyes from someone who just entered the shortlist, to someone who is in discussion as their top-three, and ending up that one person who everyone liked enough to offer them the job.

"Why are you leaving your current job?"

As a career coach myself I've been discussing the interview questions that the people I'm working with have been receiving as part of the screening application forms and at the interviews, and the interesting trend that I think its emerging in 2020 is that we see this question appear less and less often.

This could be due to the fact that priorities of the employers have shifted and the reasons for leaving previous jobs became less relevant than the display of personality that the applicants are now encouraged to lead with, plus their verifiable good track of prior work experience taking the center stage.

I'd still say that this question is likely to pop up at one point during the rounds of your interviews and preparing for it is better than ignoring it and hoping you won't have to explain yourself.

Answering this question can be tricky, and your mileage will vary greatly here.

Your real reason for leaving your previous job could be your boredom, feeling underpaid, undervalued, or even just being harassed by someone and your manager not being able to provide a safe working environment for you.

These are some of the frequently recurring real life scenarios that reflect true circumstances that drove people out of their previous jobs. Having said that, a lot of these reasons could be classified as "interview-unfriendly".

What do I mean by this?

While I'd always suggest that you say truthful and ethical in your self-presentation to the recruiters and potential employers, I'd be lying to you if I didn't acknowledge the existence of a certain *"game"* that we have to play if we want to successfully pass through the recruitment process.

The rules of this game are very simple – regardless of how truthful you'd like to be; you need to find a way to save any *heavy stuff* for later.

Remember that the interview is your self-pitch. The potential employer needs to remain positive and excited about "buying" you as a valuable Product.

Leading your self-presentation with the details about your past that are guaranteed to dampen the mood or cast a shadow over your previous employer – *whether or not they've done something severely wrong by you* – is not something that would help you stand out or get that job.

I personally hate the two-faced element of this process, and the game that I'm telling you about here, but these are just the facts we all have to deal with. As your individual circumstances are unique, I can't make a hard and fast recommendation here and only keep offering you the generic guideline, leaving the final judgment of what's "too heavy" for the interview and what's not up to you.

So what would I consider valid reasons for leaving your previous job, without ringing any alarm bells, or diving into the topic too deeply?

Here are some ideas-generating options for you:

1. *"I thought that I outgrew my previous responsibilities and wanted to shift into full-time Scrum Mastery as something I'm passionate in. My previous employer didn't offer me this option, so I had to look elsewhere..."*

2. *"As a Scrum Master I've been working with individual teams for a while, but wanted to grow professionally and join a company with mature adoption of one of the Scaled Agile frameworks, so I could keep learning."*

3. *"I heard about your company's leadership and investment into the Agile community of practice from a couple of friends of mine who used to work here, and thought it would be great to join your team for my personal and professional benefit."*

4. *"My previous job was a contract engagement, and once the project funds ran out it wasn't renewed. So I was forced to start looking."*

5. *"I decided to pivot my career and try something different after being retrenched from my previous company, and going through months of training and acting as a Scrum Master in part-time capacity."*

As you can see, I'm consciously avoiding any options that would mention any scenarios where you point out your burnout, boredom with what you've been doing, or the conflict you've been running away from.

Do not expose any heavy stuff to the interview panel and thank me later!

"What do you like to do in your spare time?"

A lot of recruiters who I talk to and the people I'm mentoring mentioned to me that this question is still coming up regularly during the interviews, although I'll be honest that I personally didn't encounter it too often.

My recommendation here would align with what I said earlier when we've covered whether or not you should include your hobbies on your CV.

Slightly different angle here however would be that you should not try and come across as someone who dedicates all of their free time to studying Agile books and YouTube videos, trying to grow as a professional.

This might be one of the things you do in your spare time, and you might even mention that, but I'd always lead here with something that most people would perceive as a hobby that makes you human and allows you to distract yourself from the work topics.

People who ask this question want to simply ensure that you have something other than work in your life, that makes you human and allows them to picture further how would it feel to work with you every day. Nobody wants someone intensely preaching them Agile on every occasion and who doesn't contribute to the nice social atmosphere they are surely trying to build or maintain within their company.

So just tell the interviewers briefly about your hobbies or what you like to do on the weekend, such as watching the latest dramas on Netflix, playing computer games or spending time with your child at the park.

"What is your biggest strength?"

If you hear this question at all, chances are you should have already had an opportunity to mention your key achievements and what makes you a great hire for this job when you've introduced yourself or answered the *"Why should we hire you?"* question.

At this stage the recruiter or the interview panel would be simply looking for the signs of your self-awareness, and the ability to highlight your strongest traits or skills without sounding like you're bragging, or being arrogant.

There could also be an element of them trying to match your claimed strengths with the required criteria for this particular job.

So for example, if you're applying for a Scrum Master role within Scaled Agile environment – *it won't hurt you to do a Google search for what that really means, by the way, as describing that is out of scope for this book* – you could reply with mentioning your particular efficiency when working with the multiple Scrum Teams that need extra efforts coordinating and syncing up their efforts, working well under pressure.

If you however think that the interview panel would be interested to hear that your biggest strength is your Karate black belt, you might be setting yourself up for a major disappointment.

"What is your biggest weakness?"

This question comes up in many forms even more frequently than the one where you are asked about your strengths.

The interviewers often want to see your ability to recognize your weaker points, as we all have some. This highlights your ability to be reasonably self-critical but positive and determined to overcome these shortfalls, preferably with a system or plan of actions that allows you to work on those weaker points and get better.

Do not think that a cheesy answer that very clearly tries hard to turn a weakness into a strength would fly well anywhere in 2020! So the answers along the lines of *"I work too much!"* should never be used, and you can surely come up with something better than that.

As with the other common interview questions, I recommend preparing an answer that doesn't sound try-hard and appears as natural and sincere as possible.

It is best to mention an actual weakness that is not critically opposite to the requirements of a Scrum Master job.

So where the answer *"I actually hate working with people…"* would certainly fly like a lead balloon, something like *"I sometimes have difficulty managing my time, but I'm conscious and working on it with the help of reminders and schedules"* would work perfectly fine.

"Describe a difficult situation you've been in, and how you've resolved it?"

One of the most common behavioral questions, this one needs to be prepared for without a doubt, and having more than one example scenario ready would be even better for you.

Answering this question, you should sound as genuine and clear as possible, describing the situation itself, how it affected you directly or indirectly, how you've analyzed what was going on, formed a plan of action, and followed it through to successful closure.

While telling the story try not to sound like the Superman.

You can show vulnerability to the interviewers, as it only makes you more human in their eyes, but be conscious of keeping the story on track where you remain in the driver's seat the whole time, taking ownership of your actions and having a clear purpose.

As with the previously suggested approach where we spare the interview panel any "heavy details", try and avoid sharing any excessive drama at this point.

Practice moving through the prepared response smoothly when talking about it, without dwelling on the negative details. Your examples don't have to be all happy and fluffy, as otherwise they won't come across as genuinely difficult situations, but remember that the Scrum Master is expected to be a good communicator and the influencer of positive change.

Not someone who engages in interpersonal squabbles or company politics. So basically, even when describing something challenging that you've been affected by personally or helping your colleagues through, try and not sound negative.

Make sure you are specific enough about how you've helped resolve the difficult situation in a positive way, stressing the fact that difficult situations are usually a learning experience for everyone.

"What qualities should a good Scrum Master possess?"

I would get the acknowledgment of great knowledge of Scrum Framework and Agile principles and values out of the way quickly, and then focus on core behaviors we as Scrum Masters would try and foster among the team members.

These would include general positivity and trusting your people to do their best to deliver value to the customer, flexibility when it comes to inevitable changes in the scope of work or team composition, empathy, transparency, and natural inclination to lead by example.

It's generally not recommended to answer this question by simply describing yourself here, and staying focused on what the Scrum Master is normally expected to do – working well with others, being patient as we have to repeat ourselves many times as we train and coach people, being generally a positive driver of cultural change.

"Where do you see yourself in 5 years?"

This question is more popular among traditional organizations and old-school HR recruitment panels, such as Government establishments and not-for-profits.

Put simply, you could generally answer this question however you like, but would do well to tweak your answer depending on the insights you've gathered by now about the culture of the company and general mood of the people around the room.

So a younger start-up that appears happy and people-centric might respond better to your aspirations being around your family, and reducing the amount of work hours so you could spend more time with your children or development of your side-business.

While a more old-school bank or insurance company interview panel that appears quite formal and less warm throughout the whole chat with you would be probably more responsive to your desire of career growth, taking up more responsibility, or considering Agile Coaching as one of the perceived natural career progression paths for the Scrum Masters.

Regardless of how exactly you've decided to answer this question, make sure you don't make it sound like the hiring organization will clearly be just a "stepping stone" for you, before you move on to something bigger and better.

Even if that is the case, your whole self-pitch should be about your passion about joining this particular company and growing within it, investing yourself in their vision and overall direction that your prior research should offer you.

Finally, it's worth mentioning that not many people would expect a job applicant to have a detailed plan of their future career or life in general, or that they'd be comfortable to reveal every detail to them at this stage.

Just make sure you sound genuine, friendly and honest, that you have a goal and general direction in life, which should be more than enough to move past this question smoothly enough.

"Do you have any questions for us?"

You should definitely prepare some, as part of your company research and interview preparation. The last thing you'd want is to come across disinterested, complacent, clueless or desperate.

Signs of your desperation could manifest themselves differently, but having no questions for the interview panel could certainly contribute to the first three of the negative images mentioned above.

This question could be seen as *"What do you know about our company?"*, where a truly motivated job seeker would surely want to capitalize on the opportunity to learn more and talk to the real people about it, rather than continue fishing for information on the Internet.

Unless the interviewers have already answered these questions, the following examples should give you some ideas to work with:

1. *"What is the average size of your Scrum teams?"*

2. *"Have there been any reports of the teams struggling with Business as Usual work interfering with their Sprint commitments?"*

3. *"Are your Business stakeholders properly engaged by the Product Owner? Do they attend your Sprint Review sessions?"*

4. *"Is the company open to sponsoring certifications or professional training programs for their employees, including Scrum Masters?"*

5. *"Are all of your Scrum teams located on-shore or some of them are based off-shore?"*

What are the Behavioral Questions?

I've given you an example of a Behavioral Question in the previous section, as the interview panels love throwing those at their job applicants.

The premise for asking those questions is the general belief that the past behavior of people largely indicates how they'd be likely to behave in the future.

Everyone understands that there is room for improvement, but a grown person is a complex human being with long-lived patterns that are unlikely to change overnight, even if they want to, influencing their actions, responses and situational judgment.

This is why many recruiters and interview panels actually limit the number of less meaningful questions like *"Where do you see yourself in 5 years?"* and fill up the valuable time with more specific and technical, or behavioral questions.

The usual goal of carefully selected behavioral questions is to identify "core behaviors" of their job candidates. If you look carefully at many job ads posted on LinkedIn and other sites, lots of those contain a section towards the bottom that talks about key qualities that their company values, or even more specifically – the expected behaviors that they expect any of their employees to exhibit.

As we are talking about Scrum Master role and responsibilities in this book, we could probably safely assume that the core behaviors your potential employers would look for would include:

1. Team leadership skills, where you'd take charge of the process where required, showing people the way and leading by example;

2. Being positively assertive and not shy to tell people what they need to know, repeating the message confidently where required;

3. Being empathetic and emotionally intelligent, which in this context would mean being able to listen to the problems that other team members might be experiencing, understanding those without passing hard judgment, and helping people work through their frustrations, connecting them with more qualified help if that need arises;

4. Resilience to stress and ability to keep steering the ship in the right direction, even under pressure of deadlines or misbehaving Business stakeholders;

5. Being confident and determined in the benefits of implementing Agile methodologies and Scrum specifically for the applicable project delivery, but not too overzealous to suggest that one-size-fits-all approach would work everywhere.

You should use the points made above to decide if you could enter that interview with some prepared examples of your past work that would address the ranges of behavioral questions that could be phrased very differently, but would ultimately try and determine that you possess what we've listed above.

Additionally, I'll offer you a few behavioral questions that I've either asked myself at an interview, or was told about by the other people attending similar Agile role interviews over the past couple of years.

1. "Please describe a stressful situation or Team environment that you've been in. How did you handle it?"

2. "How do you feel about situations where things are out of your control. Have you been in those before and how did you handle yourself?"

3. "Imagine that your team has shipped a Product Increment with a critical fault. Would you feel any responsibility for this failure? How would you suggest that your Scrum team handles the extra work to fix the issue, and the general feedback from the frustrated Business stakeholders?"

4. "As a Scrum Master in any of your previous roles, have you ever seen a Product Owner cancel a Sprint? What kind of effect did it have on team morale and how did you help handle this situation?"

5. "As a Scrum Master in any of your previous roles, did you ever have to sell the whole idea of Agile approach to the less cooperative and

traditionally-inclined Business stakeholders? How did you handle this? Please give specific examples."

6. "Have you ever been pressed for timely delivery of certain Product Features by the Project Managers when not all the requirements were clear, or the Product Backlog Items were not sufficiently refined? How did you handle this situation as a Scrum Master?"

7. "How do you approach removal of any impediments for your team as a Scrum Master? Do you have a specific example where you had to do it? Could you talk us through your approach step by step?"

8. "As a Scrum Master in any of your previous roles, did you ever have to resolve a conflict between the members of your Scrum team? What was your approach like?"

9. "Did you ever have to look at multiple teams with different Sprint Goals at the same time? What methods did you use to organize yourself to handle this situation better?"

As you can see, there's a healthy mix of behavioral and technical elements in the selection of questions above. Questions like these are going to push you through your paces a lot more than the common basic ones that we've discussed at the start of this chapter.

Human behaviors are complex and individual, which is why answering these questions becomes harder to script or predict exactly how the interview panel would steer those to get to know your limits better.

You should keep in mind that the more obvious is the hybrid nature of the role you've applied for, the broader the range of topics the interviewers might try and cover with their questions. In other words, it is always easier to be successful with job applications and the interview process for clearly defined roles that have little or no hybrid elements.

Collaboration Tools You Use

Scrum Masters aren't explicitly required to be advocates for any particular tools that automate collaboration, or any other part of our Agile work. After all, Agile Manifesto that we all embraced at some point tells us to put *Individuals and Interactions over Processes and Tools*...

When I talk about *"tools"* in this chapter, I specifically mean electronic collaboration tools that the teams use to communicate with each other, document actions, and visualize work.

Even without Scrum Master role emphasis on the tools, we need those to perform our roles effectively these days, and I do not know of many modern organizations that have no collaboration suites, still solely relying on the physical boards with some index cards and post-it notes on them.

I mean, smaller and closely-knit teams often choose to have some form of a physical board present in their team space, but majority of the organizations would have an electronic collaboration tool of sorts.

And it is not uncommon for the Scrum Master or another Agile champion of the area to become the go-to person when it comes to issuing recommendations or showing some form of prior experience with the collaboration tool that the company uses.

What does it mean for you as a Scrum Master job candidate?

You need to research and develop your own understanding of what tools are most commonly used by the Agile teams these days on the market, so that when asked, you could appear educated and proficient at least with one or two, rather than completely unprepared.

I haven't explicitly included any questions about the collaboration tools in the section where we've discussed the interview questions, but these are not uncommon either.

To refrain from copy-pasting some publicly available information about the most frequently used collaboration solutions into this book, I'll just give you a list of those I think you should invest your time into researching and playing with in your own time.

You'd do well then to Google further information and subscribe for free trials where possible – *as not all of these tools would offer a free trial to an individual* – to build up your confidence before facing the people who will expect you to show them some expertise in online collaboration, or even hoping that you'd lead that practice for their company.

Collaboration tools worthy of your attention:

1. Atlassian JIRA;

2. Trello, recently acquired by Atlassian;

3. Monday.com;

4. Asana;

5. Slack.

This list is certainly not exhaustive like any other I'm offering you in this book.

But for a brand new Scrum Master these five should be more than enough to present yourself as someone with real value to the hiring organization, who could recommend and share their experience with some of the most commonly used tools on the project delivery market of 2020.

The arguments in favor of digital Agile Boards

As I've already mentioned in the section above, some of the companies and Agile communities of practice try and stay more "purist" in their approach and do things by the classic book, frowning upon decentralized Scrum team setups and only recognizing physical Agile Boards – *often interchangeably referred to as Agile Walls* – as the right way to collaborate and visualize work.

You might even be asked by the potential employer what type of Boards do you prefer and why, as part of your meet and greet, or the interview process.

Sharing my own opinion with you here I'd say that it's a bit silly to deny the fact that in the modern distributed and interconnected world that evolves and utilizes the new methods of communication and collaboration, we as true agilists have to stick to the traditional physical Scrum Board setup to feel like we are doing the right thing.

We champion change in the organizations and individuals, yet appear stubborn in accepting that the world around us is changing and we need to evolve our own understanding of what became an acceptable and good practice, when we set up a Scrum process ourselves.

So if you find yourself in the need to provide arguments in favor of adopting a digital collaboration platform and an Agile Board of sorts, you could fall back on the following reasons:

1. Contribution to distributed – *even cross-continental* – accessibility of the required information for all the Scrum team members;

2. Collaboration tools have evolved, and there are plenty to choose from to satisfy the needs of your Business, as opposed to limited offering 5-10 years ago;

3. We work natively in the "Digital space", where the way our team environment is set up is often not even allowing for the sufficient amount of the physical space shared by the members of the same Scrum team. And if all of your documentation and team chat history is already living in the Cloud, why should the placement or treatment of your Agile Board be any different?

4. Digital storage and organization of the Backlog items and their lifecycle directly contributes to automation of the relevant reports – Burn-down charts, Cumulative Flow Diagrams, Team Velocity Report, Portfolio View of the Backlog Epics, and others.

Attempting to track all of that valuable information with the help of a physical board, spending time to reconcile all the numbers and movement of cards, etc., would create an immense overhead of your efforts as the Scrum Master. The efforts that without a doubt could be better spent elsewhere!

Having said all of the above, making arguments in favor of digital collaboration tools and Agile Boards I'd only add that there is still an evident benefit to having some form of physical presence of that board in your Scrum team space.

No, I'm not contradicting what I've just told you above, but only suggesting that you should recommend that the team finds a way to project their digital Agile Board somehow – with the help of an actual inexpensive projector, or making use of one of the TV screens with a digital port that a PC could be connected to.

With all the appreciation of the freedom digital collaboration tools offer us in 2020, nothing beats the dynamics of standing around some type of a "Wall" and discussing work in progress while being able to physically point at the work items, especially if the external or Business observers are present.

Conclusion

I sincerely hope that I've delivered on my promise to make you a better informed and prepared candidate for Scrum Master job search and application process, at the cost of you buying me a coffee.

If I had to summarize everything I've told you in the previous chapters, I'd say – don't just decide one morning that you'd like to be a Scrum Master and start mindlessly applying for any job ad that has the words "Agile" or "Scrum" in them.

Invest some efforts into uplifting your capabilities, knowledge and the whole presentation of your professional persona in your CV and for the face-to-face conversations with the recruitment professionals and the hiring management down the track.

Do your freely accessible reading of the fundamental documents such as the Scrum Guide and the Agile Manifesto, prepare for your Scrum Master certification exam and get that badge as the minimum acceptable pass-mark for any modern Agile job applicant.

Be realistic about whether or not you can do the whole career pivot by yourself. Decide if investing a modest amount of money into hiring a Career Coach to prepare you for the journey and set you off on the right path would be worth it for you.

While I am saying this as an interested party – being someone who offers coaching services to the Agile job seekers on JoinAgile.com – I truly believe that a perspective of an unbiased external expert almost always gives the individuals a tremendous boost to their confidence.

In the case of JoinAgile Initiative we don't just condition people to be more resilient job seekers and better Agile champions at the end of the day, but connect our people with the recruitment professionals who specialize in the placement of Agile talent and would be able to take your case further.

Change is difficult for all of us. Deciding to relabel yourself as a Scrum Master or any other champion of the Agile movement is a bold move that requires personal motivation and persistence that usually pays off down the track.

I hope you've learned something useful by reading this book, and wish you all the professional success you deserve,

Other Books from JoinAgile

Writing this book and the similar content under the umbrella of my JoinAgile Initiative, I'd like you to be aware of the other publications that I've released over the past few years.

They were planned as a logical sequence of career steps and your learning efforts to become better at your craft as an Agile champion, or even to consider further transitioning to Agile Coaching.

The conditions of this eBook publication don't allow me to embed direct links to the resources that might be of interest to you, so instead I'm including the book names and their brief descriptions below, *encouraging you to visit JoinAgile.com* as a one-stop-shop that will direct you further.

It's worth mentioning that all of our publications, including eBooks and Audiobooks *are available for free* to anyone engaging in the paid Career Coaching services from JoinAgile Initiative.

"Agile Coaching: Where to start?"

If you've been working as a Scrum Master or the Product Owner, or any other Agile champion for a while, learning a lot about good and bad patterns, guiding Scrum teams on the ground for a few years, it's likely that you'd start looking at the further steps in your career progression.

One of this logical steps could be becoming an Agile Coach.

Unsurprisingly, this would be a transition of its own, requiring further investment into learning and mainly broadening your skills and knowledge far beyond the Agile Manifesto and Scrum.

"Agile Coaching: Where to start?" is available as a paperback, eBook and an Audiobook from the various online retailers, and was designed to help jump-start your Agile Coaching career, offering you some guidance on the mindset change that you'd need to consciously focus on, and a simple framework to follow as a fresh coach with not much practical experience.

This book does not talk about the particulars of the recruitment process however, and instead dives into what I believe you need to know as an aspiring Agile Coach about how we actually do our work – typical Coaching Journey we envisage by default, the recommended high-level sequence of Agile events and practices that we'd follow, and similar insights.

"Agile Ceremonies: The details you were missing"

While this book taught you the basics of career transitioning into the Agile professional space, our most recent publication – *"Agile Ceremonies: The details you were missing"* – is now available to offer you exactly what it says on the cover!

Freshly certified Scrum Masters who are thrown into action and left to take care of their teams are often lost when it comes to the right execution of Scrum ceremonies that the Scrum Guide told you about, but never really took you through any of those step by step, making sure you understand the details that usually emerge only through working in the Agile environment.

In this new book I've tried to offer you another shortcut to knowledge, offering you a solid way to start on Day One at your new job and appear informed straight away, or at least have some plan of action that would surely reduce your anxiety and fear of the unknown.

"Agile and Lean, and what do they mean?"

This book is currently available in the Audio version only, which is slightly unusual as the authors normally write a manuscript and publish the eBook or paperback and only then convert it into Audio format.

In our case the release of "Agile and Lean..." wasn't as thoroughly planned initially, and I've never expected it to become as popular as all the sales numbers have proven it to be over the course of 2019. Life is full of surprises, and some of those are pleasant, I guess?

Majority of the content of "Agile and Lean..." came as refined fragments of our old and no longer running "Lean and Mean Agile Podcast". I've received a lot of positive feedback about the topics I've been covering on the podcast back in 2016 and 2017, but the amount of work required to maintain the podcast with the new episodes needing to be released every week was too much to handle for me back then.

So the podcast was stopped, and the episodes remained accessible to the public for a couple of years. But supporting any initiative costs money and I've been seeking additional revenue streams and distribution channels that could help me spread the word about JoinAgile Initiative.

This made me record additional bits of content that would wrap the fragments of the podcast nicely together, turning those into the logical flow of a book-like narrative, which ended up becoming the "Agile and

Lean, and what do they mean" audiobook.

If you've missed out on our podcast back in the day, and would like to build general awareness about what Agile and Lean Thinking are all about, with the core values, principles, ceremonies, roles, interactions and so forth being explained to you in an easy and conversational way – then you'd probably enjoy and benefit from finding this book on the Audiobook retailer website of your choice!

JoinAgile on YouTube

Most of JoinAgile social media presence has shifted from the podcast, LinkedIn and Twitter feeds to YouTube these days.

If you are interested in the previews of our Audiobook chapters, announcements of the new services, giveaways and discounts, as well as standalone videos talking about the variety of topics relevant to Agile job seekers and the existing practitioners – please consider finding us on YouTube and subscribing to the channel.

Feedback

Your feedback, content requests and suggestions are of the highest importance to me as the author of this book and the founder of JoinAgile Initiative.

It is what helped me maintain my motivation to keep writing and publishing content that my readers and YouTube channel subscribers have been consuming so far, helping JoinAgile grow over the years in terms of both content and the service offerings.

I'm always happy to hear from my readers and fellow Agile practitioners, so please connect to me on LinkedIn, follow JoinAgile on YouTube, and visit JoinAgile.com for the variety of contact options that you're welcome to use.

I always respond to anyone who showed their support by bothering to connect and write a few lines of constructive feedback or wishes.

About the Author

Dmitri is a Business Transformation Leader and Agile Career Coach, passionate about the New Ways of Working and Digital Disruption, helping companies define and implement the new operating models and optimization strategies to remain competitive and Customer-focused in the modern business landscape.

Pragmatic and hands-on Lean-Agile practitioner, Dmitri introduces all the necessary concepts and hybrid models with the required blend of the elements that set the foundation for a longer-term digital transformation, enabling faster feedback loops, empirical planning, reduction of risk, and more sustainable pace of value delivery to the Customer.

Published author and the founder of JoinAgile Initiative, helping the aspiring Agile practitioners grow professionally, and the recruiters to find the right Lean-Agile talent, using the new and advanced professional competency testing system.

Copyright

Copyright © 2016 - 2020 by Dmitri Iarandine. All rights reserved.

This book or any portion thereof may not be reproduced or used in any manner whatsoever without the express written permission of the Author.

www.JoinAgile.com

hello@joinagile.com

www.ingramcontent.com/pod-product-compliance
Lightning Source LLC
Chambersburg PA
CBHW031423210526
45464CB00005B/2030